C000259744

YOUR CRAFT BUSINESS
A STEP-BY-STEP GUIDE

Also by
KEVIN PARTNER

How to set up an Online Business

Your Craft Business
A Step by Step Guide

KEVIN PARTNER

This edition first published 2012

Published by Scribbleit.

Scribbleit Ltd, 17 Brightside, Waterlooville, Hampshire, PO7 7BA, United Kingdom

First Edition, October 2012

ISBN: 978-0-9574516-2-9

Copyright

Copyright © 2012 Kevin Partner. All rights reserved.

The right of the author to be identified as the author of this work has been asserted in accordance with the Copyright, Designs and Patents Act 1988.

All rights reserved. No part of this publication may be reproduced, stored in a retrieval system, or transmitted, in any form or by any means, electronic, mechanical, photocopying, recording or otherwise, except as permitted by the UK Copyright, Designs and Patents Act 1988, without the prior permission of the publisher.

Disclaimer

Please note that this publication is intended as general guidance only and does not constitute accountancy, tax, financial or any other professional advice. The author and Scribbleit Ltd make no representations or warranties with respect to the accuracy of completeness of the contents of this publication and cannot accept any responsibility for any liability, loss or risk, personal or otherwise which may arise, directly or indirectly, from reliance on information contained in this publication. You are recommended to seek accountancy, tax, financial and other professional advice from a suitably qualified individual familiar with your personal circumstances.

FOR PETA

Contents

About the Author

Kevin Partner started his first business in 1999 and currently owns four companies including, with his wife Peta, craft retailer MakingYourOwnCandles.co.uk

Since 1995, Kevin has been a Contributing Editor of PC Pro, the UK's leading technology magazine. He currently writes a monthly column covering Online Business.

Kevin is also the author of "How to set up an online business", published by Dennis Publishing and currently in its fourth edition.

About the Website

This book has a supporting website – **www.yourcraftbusiness.co.uk** – which contains all the links and other resources mentioned. If you're reading this on an ebook reader, then it's best to go to the website on a computer or tablet and click the links from there.

PREFACE

Back in April 2009, Peta and I were cuddled up on the sofa watching *Kirstie's Homemade Home*. The lovely Kirstie Allsopp had spent the episode making candles. I was in the early stages of writing "How to set up an online business"[1] and was looking for an idea for a new business so that I could develop it alongside writing the book. There were several in the frame at the time, including "veg in a bucket", "a puzzle a day" and a training site to help people pass the UK citizenship test.

Kirstie seemed to enjoy making candles and it didn't look too difficult. At first glance, we thought it might make a business that would suit us both – candle making seemed to me to be as close to chemistry as I was ever likely to be allowed in the kitchen and it appealed to Peta's creative side.

So, we marched to Hobbycraft that Saturday and bought a Candle Making Starter Kit by House of Crafts. We brought it home, opened it and were immediately disappointed by how little we'd got for our money. Rattling around inside the box was a very small bag of wax, some wick, some dye in bizarre little paint pots and cheap looking moulds that had been punched out of plastic – I was even expected to drill my own holes! The results were predictably awful.

Many of the best business ideas come out of frustration – so we decided to find out whether it was possible to design our own kits (having found that no-one else did this) that would allow customers to make candles of a consistently high quality, at a fair price that would enable us to make a reasonable profit. Six months of experimenting and setup later, we launched a pilot version of our online shop with just three products – the Basic, Professional and Deluxe Candle Making Kits. We ran the "popup" online shop over November and into December and it did well enough in the Christmas rush to convince us it might become a profitable business.

We spent a busy New Year adding products and finding a good online shop package – and relaunched in early January 2010. And we haven't

---

[1]   Available from Amazon.co.uk and on Kindle.

looked back.

MakingYourOwnCandles has been a wonderful success. Not only because it provides a full time income for Peta, which meant she didn't have to find a part time job when our son started school, but also because we absolutely love it. We enjoy creating new products and seeing which ones our customers like, we love the interactions we have with our friends on our Facebook Page but above all, we get a massive thrill at every email, status update or review from a customer as they tell us how much they've enjoyed our products (and Peta's world famous customer service) or made money from them.

We dedicate this book to the customers of MakingYourOwnCandles.co.uk – and we hope that some of you will be inspired to create your own craft businesses whether that's in candle making, soap making, card making, brownie making or any other form of craft.

We think craft customers are a wonderful community who have been badly served by the big retailers. They're crying out for high quality, good value products – can you provide them? Why not find out?

ABOUT THIS BOOK

In 2009, I wrote a book called "How to set up an online business" for Dennis Publishing. Since then, it's gone on to sell out each of the three print runs so far and is currently in its fourth edition. More than anything else, I've been thrilled by the responses from readers – both in the form of emails and reviews on Amazon and elsewhere. The book has appeared in printed form in book shops and supermarkets across the UK (it was a thrill and a half to see it for the first time in my local Sainsbury's a few years ago!) and has also been sold in the US, Canada, Australia and, in its Kindle edition, across the world.

Readers told me they particularly appreciated the very specific, in-depth, often step-by-step advice I gave. This was heartening because I'd set out to do that – I'd been frustrated by the lack of detail in the business books I'd read. They were a bit like printed popcorn-enjoyable to read but, after half an hour, they leave you hungry and wondering what to eat next.

Since that book was written, Peta and I have been running **www.MakingYourOwnCandles.co.uk**. The biggest surprise for us was the warmth and enthusiasm of the crafting community - it genuinely gives us a thrill to be involved with such a wonderful group of people. We're also constantly amazed by the creative ways in which our products are used. Frankly, we often see candles posted on our Facebook Page (**http://fb.com/MakingYourOwnCandles**) that put our efforts to shame!

So we know you're a creative, intelligent, hard working crowd. We also know, from the response we received when we suggested writing this book, that many of you want to start making money from your talents.

We've been around the craft community for long enough to know that **you have what it takes** to make a success of your business. What you need is straightforward, specific, advice that pulls no punches and answers the questions you've asked, not what an author might *imagine you want to know.*

This book is for you. I'm going to take you into the heart of real world business and show you how to do it, in practice. We will go into unprecedented depth on the topics crafters have told us are most important but we will do it step by step. And at the end of it, you'll have a business.

With a little money (many craft business can establish themselves on a budget of less than £100) and the talent and determination you already have, you can create a profitable business in next to no time.

I have faith in you. All I ask is that you believe in yourself, strap yourself in, grab a notebook and enjoy the ride.

And if you have any questions or suggestions – email me at **kev@yourcraftbusiness.co.uk**

Kev Partner

CHAPTER 1: INTRODUCTION

In September 2012, we asked 1,000 customers of MakingYourOwnCandles.co.uk what they would like to know about starting a craft business of their own. This book answers their questions, and many more besides. If you want nitty-gritty, you're in the right place.

BUSINESS 101

Creating your own successful craft business from home is not rocket science. To be profitable, a business needs to do four things:

1. create a desirable product

2. place that product in front of an appropriate audience

3. sell and deliver it to that audience for more than it costs to make

4. whilst operating efficiently and within the law.

And that's it. Everything else is just huff, fluff and puff. Granted, there's quite a lot to say about each of these and that's what this book is about – but I want you to remember what our purpose is when setting up a business: to make something, tell people about it and sell it to them for a profit.

This book contains specific, practical advice for crafters setting up business in the UK. As well as product development, marketing, production and sales, I look at UK tax and company regulations since many people have told me they're particularly bothered by the man in the bowler hat.

I recommend reading the book from cover to cover if you're a newcomer to business. If you've already set up and you're looking for specific advice, by all means dip in and out as you wish.

WHAT'S STOPPING YOU?

The chances are, you've been thinking about starting a craft business for a while. After all, making money from something you love doing is a common enough dream. So, why aren't we all living that dream already? Here are some of the reasons most often given:

"I don't know what's involved"

"I don't know where to begin"

"What if the business fails?"

"I'm not sure my crafting/business skills are good enough"

"I don't want to take a financial risk"

"I don't feel like a businessperson – do I look like Alan Sugar?"

"I don't have time"

I can help you with all but the final one in this list. I'm not Hermione Granger, I don't have a time turner that will magically allow you to be in two places at once. This may seem unsympathetic but "I don't have time" is one of the weakest excuses for not starting your business. If your days are truly stuffed with essential activities (and I appreciate that, for some people, this is true), then put down this book until you can devote a little time every day to your ambitions.

For most of us, though, lack of time is an excuse. It's amazing how we can magically find the time when push comes to shove, when a task gets promoted up the priority list so that it's given its due weight.

Here's an example. This book has been in the planning for a long time and I'd marked up a period in my diary to get it written based on how quickly I write (I've been writing professionally for nearly 20 years so this wasn't too difficult to estimate). And then, typically, another writing assignment was dropped on me with a very tight deadline. My choices were either to postpone this book for 6 months, or get it written in the much shorter slot now available to me.

The fact that you're reading this now, shows that I did it – to my usual exacting standards. How did I do it? By working long hours and side-lining lower priority work, however much I'd been looking forward to it.

I am not pretending for one moment that, for some people, fitting a business into their current life is impossible. What I am saying is that for many of us (me included), it's an excuse our subconscious offers up to protect us from the potential for failure.

THE "F" WORD

Let's get this out in the open right at the beginning - failure is a part of business. In fact, without failure you're extremely unlikely to succeed. However, if your image of "failure" is of the bailiffs carting off your knitting machine, think again.

Let's say I create a new product and rent a stall at a local craft fair. I do a great job of laying out my stall professionally, my product looks good and I've priced competitively. But I don't sell a thing.

Is that a failure? Most people would say it was – and I certainly don't recommend deliberately trying to sell nothing. However, in fact this exercise was only a failure if you learned nothing from it. During the day, you'll have had the chance to speak to dozens, perhaps hundreds, of potential customers. They'll have picked up your product, had a look at it, maybe a sniff or two, before putting it down again.

Even if you don't feel confident enough to talk to them directly (and this is a skill you'll acquire with practice, I promise) you'll be able to tell from their body language and anything they say to their companions, what they thought about your product. One way or another, you should leave the fair with a very clear idea how you need to change the product, its packaging or whatever – so that next time you will sell. In other words, your craft "disaster" turned out to be a "triumph" of market research.

When Peta and I attended our first fair as stall-holders we only sold a couple of kits. Financially, on the day at least, it was a "failure". However, we learned many things (for example, the importance of waterproof labels!) - including that visitors to craft fairs are more likely to buy candles than candle kits. In other words, we'd been totally wrong, but we learned a valuable lesson.

One of the keys to a successful business is to separate the viable ideas and products from those that are not commercially credible – and to do this as early as possible. It may seem counter-intuitive but accepting that some of your inspirations are going to fail is a very important step in preventing the business itself from failing. If you open yourself up to the idea that not every product is an act of genius, you will then listen to your customers as they tell you exactly what they do want.

So, you need to focus on learning rather than earning in the early days. Watch a young child as they attempt to learn a new skill – whether it's standing up for the first time or solving a puzzle. Young kids are not afraid to fail – if they were, they'd never take their first step. Be that child, don't take it personally, and learn, learn, learn. Ironically, this is the quickest way to a successful business.

THE "E" WORD/WHAT IF IT FAILS?/FINANCIAL RISK

No, you're not Alan Sugar, and thank heavens for that – one is enough. You're not Deborah Meaden or Theo Paphitis either. These entrepreneurs are exceptional and they play by different, and dangerous, rules. For every Richard Branson there are thousands who've tried to follow his path, betting everything and losing the same.

But for every Branson, there are also tens of thousands of business owners who make a good living following low-risk strategies. It's a myth that all businesses need bank lending secured on their house – you should never risk what you can't afford to lose and I've never risked my home. I want to reassure you that starting a craft business at home doesn't have to involve any risk beyond a small amount of money (you decide how much). The main investment you make in your new venture is time and that's what you have to lose if it doesn't work out.

The real risk is surely the regret you'll feel if you never give it a go?

I DON'T KNOW WHERE TO BEGIN/I DON'T KNOW WHAT'S INVOLVED

Read on. This book is aimed at complete newcomers to business – by the time you've finished it, you'll know exactly what you need to do in order to create a successful business at home.

I'M NOT SURE MY CRAFTING/BUSINESS SKILLS ARE GOOD ENOUGH

Becoming proficient in your craft is simply a matter of practice (if you don't believe me, I recommend Malcolm Gladwell's book "Outliers", it's an eye-opener). Whilst it's true that some people are born with better hand-eye coordination than others and that this changes as we age, you'll find that the best proponents of your particular craft are also those that practice it the most.

When will you know if you've reached a "professional" level? Well, one good clue is that people buy from you! My advice is not to worry – you're likely to be your own harshest critic. By all means visit your local craft fair and look at what other people in your field are selling, you may be surprised, especially if you look closely!

As for business skills – that's what this book is here for. You don't need to study for an MBA to run a successful business (indeed, an MBA would probably be a hindrance), it's more a matter of being organised and having staying-power. And reading this book, of course.

LET'S GET STARTED

In summary, then – if you're good with your hands, willing to learn, prepared to work hard and get organised, and if you have a little time available, you can do it. Mix in a little creative flair and a willingness to try new things and you could well have a success on your hands. It's time to start the car and get going!

Case Study: Elaine Stavert from Littlecote Soap Co. (www.littlecotesoap.co.uk)

Tell us about your business

> *"The Littlecote Soap Co. produce handmade natural soaps, toiletries and scented products and are based on a working farm in the Buckinghamshire countryside, a short walk from my home. We are now in our 9th year and employ 8 staff to hand-make and hand-package our products which are sold in Gift Shops, National Trust, Stately Homes and Garden Centres throughout the UK. I am also the author of 5 Craft books on how to make natural toiletries."*

What inspired you to start a business?

> *"My husband and I moved out of the city to a newly converted barn in the countryside next to a farm. I wanted a part time job, but couldn't find anything interesting locally, and it was while on holiday at a market in France that I saw a rainbow of wonderful soaps on a craft stall, had my "eureka" moment, and decided to make and sell natural soap inspired by my surrounding countryside and plants."*

Case Study: Anita Street of Say It With Brownies (www.sayitwithbrownies.co.uk)

Tell us about your business

"My business is called Say It With Brownies and I sell gift boxes of chocolate brownies online that are posted to your door. I am based on the Isle of Wight and work from my kitchen at home. The idea is that people can send a box of brownies instead of a greetings card or a bunch of flowers. Through my website, you can select one of seventeen different messages to customise your gift box with choices including Happy Birthday, Thank You, With Love, Baby Boy or Thinking of You. Just like when you order flowers, I have a gift card and you say what you'd like to have handwritten onto it. The brownies themselves come in six different flavours with White Chocolate Chip Brownies and Chunky Fudge Brownies being the most popular. You get a dozen good size brownies which will keep any chocoholic happy for a couple of days!"

What inspired you to start a business?

"I was at the stage in my career when I needed a change. I loved the idea of having the freedom to be my own boss and experience the highs and lows that go with it. My husband and I decided it was time to move from Hertfordshire and that was the perfect opportunity for a complete change of lifestyle. So we sold up and moved to the island, allowing me to have the opportunity to create something of my own."

Chapter 2: You and Your Business

Why are you going into business? It's important to have a goal, or a mind's-eye view of the future so you can set your expectations, and those of the people around you, to a sensible level.

First of all – who is going to benefit from the enterprise? Most people start their own business to either supplement or replace their current sources of income. Some people want to generate revenue for a local charity, school or whatever. Either way, the aim is to make sure that whoever is set to benefit (you, your family or your local primary school) gets the maximum net income from your activities – to do this, you must act like a business.

In general, the best approach is to start small and grow gently. There are a couple of reasons for this. Firstly, the smaller you are, the less costly (and the less public) your mistakes are. Get it right first, and then expand. Secondly, by starting with the aim of creating a modest additional income, you're not going to have to spend much, avoiding the need to ask your local bank to grant you an overdraft or loan [1].

Once you have a business that's generating a profit, you can look at how you crank it up so that it replaces all or part of your income.

Now, for some of you, the idea of being able to give up your current job to work on your craft full time might seem like a pipe dream but it is genuinely achievable – Peta and I have done it with MakingYourOwnCandles, a business that started from nothing and has grown without any bank finance. On the other hand, some of you have no such ambition and are happy to supplement your income. In the early stages, the only difference is that if you have ambitions to replace a full time income, you must pick a marketplace that will ultimately be able to support it.

Some people go into business with the aim of selling their company in the future. This is usually a mistake, especially with craft businesses, partly because if you chase money in that way you'll probably never catch it, and partly because craft businesses rely on your skills (or those of your employees) and so they're relatively difficult to make large enough to become worth the sort of 5 or 6 figure value many people dream of.

---

[1]   In the unlikely event they said "yes", they'd probably charge an outrageous fee

However, there's nothing wrong with having half an eye on the long term value of your company. Again, you'll need to bear it in mind when you decide which market to enter.

For now, we need to concentrate on getting up and running. For that you'll need the following:

- Time

- Space (and a Tardis too, if you can manage it!)

- Tech

- Motivation

- A little cash

- Skill

- Dedication

TIME

The more time you can devote to your business, the quicker you'll get up and running. For some people, it's easier to find an hour a day than 7 hours once a week but, either way, you need to have dedicated time when you won't be disturbed. Starting a business involves keeping several balls in the air at once and if your mind is elsewhere it's all too likely you'll drop one – with potentially expensive implications. A small amount of concentrated time is better than several hours when you're distracted or tired.

SPACE

You need space to make your craft products and separate space from which to run your business. If you have a garage you can use, so much the better as you'll be able to properly separate business and home – similarly if there's a corner of the garden shed you can liberate. The kitchen table is the classic craft business location, but the sheer hassle of having to clear away every day is likely to grate after a while. If you're really lucky, you'll have a spare room you can use but a corner of the main bedroom is often all that's needed

TECH

Much of your research, administration, order fulfilment, stock ordering etc will be done online. You don't need a top of the line computer – a basic laptop is ideal as you can lug it from place to place. I'll cover this in more detail later in the book but please bear in mind that a tablet (for example iPad, Kindle Fire HD, Nexus 7) is no substitute for a laptop.

MOTIVATION

What will keep you going when your energy flags? This is why it's so important to have a clear understanding of why you're starting your business. Even if you don't intend to go full time, just think about what an extra £500 per month (£6,000 per year) would do for you, your family, or your chosen beneficiary.

Always keep your goals in mind when you're working, especially when doubt creeps up on you. Set up small rewards for achieving steps along the way, for example registering with HMRC, to make sure you finish every task you start. Your business is an extension of you so it deserves everything you've got.

CASH

Whilst a lot can be achieved with free resources, it's next to impossible to start up a business on a budget of zero. However, the investment needed (beyond your normal crafting budget) is pretty small. Up to a point, a larger pot of initial money will mean you can get started more quickly but it really isn't necessary to spend your life savings.

How much is "pretty small"? It depends on your business. With MakingYourOwnCandles we had to buy in some stock and that's where most of our initial investment went. Overall, including extensive market research, I reckon we spent around £400. We could probably have done it for half that if we'd been willing to slow down the launch of the business but that would have meant missing the crucial Christmas period, and would therefore have cost more than it saved.

On the other hand, if you were starting a business selling made candles, the initial investment could be little more than a **bulk container candle kit**, some labels and the cost of a table at a craft fair.

Where should the money come from? If you're not in the happy position of having savings you can use then one option is to lend money from a credit card to the business. Remember, we're talking about small amounts.

If this isn't an option, could you consider asking a family member? I appreciate that this works better with some families than others!

You can consider seeking private investment from a businessperson but this will be hard to come by and you shouldn't, under any circumstances, give away any ownership of your company in exchange. I've experienced the nightmare of carrying "sleeping" partners who contribute nothing to the business and make it harder for you to make a profit.

Finally, if you're up for a challenge and you have no other source, you could try approaching your bank. You will almost certainly be asked to "guarantee" any borrowing. This is not the same as securing an overdraft on your house but still needs to be taken seriously- seek legal advice if you're at all unsure.

SKILL

You need to develop three skills – those of the *technician, the manager* and the *entrepreneur.*

You're probably a pretty competent technician already – you can probably turn out a good product. You might not have complete confidence but that comes with practice and experience. You can create a professional product that people will pay for and should never let a perceived lack of technical skill put you off. Practice, practice, practice.

The manager is the part of you that runs the business – that makes sure the right regulations are followed, that your online shop is working and fully stocked and that orders go out on time. If you've organised a household or had any sort of administrative job, you have all the skills you need.

Finally, the one most people are frightened of. The entrepreneur, in a nutshell, is the part of you that looks out over the rim of the trench and gazes into no-man's-land to see which direction you should head in. The entrepreneur is the leader, the dreamer, the person with the vision of where you're going. Without wearing your entrepreneur hat, your manager will very efficiently ensure the technician makes....the wrong product.

You'll notice I didn't include "the salesperson" in that list. That's because you don't need them, at least not in the way you might imagine.

DEDICATION
That's what you need (if you wanna be the best). To keep pushing ahead when motivation deserts you, your confidence takes a dip and there are other things that need doing, and it would be a whole lot easier to just stop now and give up on the dream. These moments will happen, they happen to all of us. "Who do I think I am to believe I can start a business? Don't be so silly!" When you hear that voice, give yourself a thorough telling-off and get your nose back to the grindstone – it's a sure sign you're getting somewhere[1].

Pushing through the collywobbles separates the business owner from the wannabe. Which are you?

---

[1] Because as you get nearer to making your business a reality, your subconscious will seek to protect you from disappointment by discouraging you. Just remember, whilst its intentions might be sincere, it would, if it could, prevent you from ever achieving anything. Tell it to go back to sleep!

WHY START A BUSINESS NOW?

I've saved this till last because this is an objection you're more likely to hear from others when you mention you're starting a business than anything you think yourself.

Isn't the economy tanking? Surely there's no money? Are you crazy?

Let's get some facts straight. Yes, the economy is struggling and, in all likelihood, there will be little change for a while yet. However, it's still roughly the size it was before the crisis hit in 2008. Some sectors are doing well, some are unchanged, others are doing poorly.

Fortunately for you, and me, the craft sector is doing very well. Why? I think there are a number of reasons. Firstly, when the media is full of grim reports spinning every new set of figures in the most negative light possible, it's nice to sit in a comfortable armchair and finish sewing the hem of your latest halloween costume ready to put it on sale in the morning.

I also think that as our everyday lives become more and more technological, more and more about moving bits of data from computer to computer, people are looking for something more hands-on for their hobbies. The simple pleasure of turning out a perfect pillar candle is so much more real than the satisfaction of finishing a spreadsheet forecast. Others, who don't want to make craft items themselves, get second-hand pleasure through buying hand made products and using them in their homes. It reminds them of simpler times and they like the uniqueness of every human-created object in a world that is increasingly generic.

Finally, many people buy craft items as a reasonably-priced way to treat themselves – in a similar way to the surge in chocolate sales Cadbury sees in difficult times for the economy. A chunk of handmade soap, a sweet smelling container candle or a personalised brownie – these things are affordable luxuries for people who want something just a little different.

So starting a craft business right now makes perfect sense. Despite all the good reasons to do it, many people hold back because they buy the media doom and gloom. This means less competition for you, if you take the plunge.

It's true that the banks are playing hard to get, that business credit cards are hard to get hold of and that shops are closing at an alarming rate. However, advertising has never been cheaper, it's never been easier or cheaper to get a short term lease on a business unit and the internet opens up wonderful opportunities to get a nationwide (or worldwide) audience for your products, not to mention new technologies that enable you to take card payments at a craft fair with nothing but a smartphone! None of these things was true when the economy was booming – now's the time to grab the bull by the horns and make the most of these "difficult" times because when things "improve", you'll be in the best possible position to exploit the extra money in the economy. After all, if MakingYourOwnCandles can do it (starting from a fold out table in the kitchen), why can't you?

WHAT ARE YOU GOING TO CALL YOUR BUSINESS?

This is a fun bit – but it's also important. If you intend to attract business through your own website or a marketplace such as Etsy, you need to think carefully about what words and phrases your potential customers are likely to use when looking for you.

For example, if you think they'll use terms such as "hand made soap" then you should seriously think of having those words in your business name. For example "Jodie's hand made soap". This applies across all crafts – don't be tempted to give yourself a "creative" name like "Amazon". I know they're one of the biggest brands in the world now but you're not Amazon! You need every advantage you can give yourself.

Case Study: MakingYourOwnCandles

I'd be the first to admit that our name is *slightly odd – perhaps "MakeYourOwnCandles" or "MakeMyOwnCandles" would have been better. However, people looking for candle making kits will use the following phrases:*

"candle making kits"

"making candles"

"candle making"

As it happens the first of these is by far the best because someone typing that in is probably interested in buying – whereas the others could easily be typed by someone researching the area or looking for free resources. So, "making" is a better choice than "make". Hence the name. Go ahead and type "candle making kit" into Google.co.uk and see who comes top!

CHAPTER 3: YOUR PRODUCT

What are you going to sell? Whatever it is you're best at? Not necessarily, not yet. Choosing the right market and the right products to make is the essential first step in creating a successful business.

THE "MYSTERY" OF BUSINESS

As I said at the beginning, business is pretty simple in principle. But then, so is learning to read, write, walk or speak a foreign language – these are all easy to grasp in principle but hard to achieve in practice. And yet, we manage to learn to read though a mixture of formal teaching and trial and error. Learning how to do business is exactly the same – it is not a mystery, there's no magical ray of light that suddenly splits the heavens and makes it all clear. Setting up and running a successful business is a process of learning step by step, always moving towards the unattainable goal of the perfect enterprise.

Have you heard of the Pareto Principle? It's also known as the "80/20 rule". In this case, what it means is that you can learn the most important 80% of what you need to know about running your business in the first 20% of the hours you spend working on it. In other words, you can get up and running, and avoid the main pitfalls, very early on. Think of this book as your guide to that first 80%.

Running a profitable business starts with developing and creating the right product, so that's where we'll begin.

GETTING IT WRONG FIRST TIME

You've probably heard about "startups" - more often than not involving internet companies. You might have an image of the early days of Facebook, or even of the archetypal "garage" startup – such as in the real world cases of HP and Apple. But you're a startup too (indeed, you might use your garage!) and you need to think the way they do at the beginning.

A startup is like a baby company and, just as with babies, we shouldn't have the same expectations of our newborn as we do of their teenage siblings. The job of a startup is to **find** a way to make a profit from its activities – the job of a mature company is to **maximise** that profit and scale it.

So your measure of success, in the early days of your business, should be how close you are to developing a profitable product line and the marketing and distribution wherewithal to get into the hands of your customers – it should not, at the beginning, be purely about how much money you're making.

Here's an example. If someone was in a tight squeeze and needed to make money quickly, I'd recommend they do one of two things. Either raid their loft (and the lofts of generous family and friends – with their permission) and sell as much as they possibly can on eBay or buy a container-full of stuff and sell it at their local market. Measured in pure financial terms, these would be profitable ideas but the first is unlikely to be sustainable in the long term (unless you have a LOT of junk!) and the second is hardly enjoyable.

So, the aim of a startup is to get to a point where you know *exactly* how to make money in your chosen market. If you're a soap-maker, then, this means you've found out which recipes, sizes, packaging and prices are the most profitable for you. Your business then leaves the startup phase and grows up – it never stops learning but now its main focus is on efficiently and profitably cranking out products that you know your market wants.

BE LEAN

This might sound a bit counter-intuitive and, indeed, the vast majority of new businesses don't start this way. It's much more typical for a new entrepreneur to settle on a product early (perhaps based on a little market research, often not), find suppliers so they can buy the raw materials in bulk, get labels printed, packaging sorted, leaflets and advertising booked, website built, craft fairs organised. You get the picture.

And then they find, to their horror, that no-one wants to buy what they have to sell, at a price they can make a profit from.[1]

This is one of the main reasons companies fail – especially early on[2]. But modern production techniques, home equipment and the wonderful internet come together to offer an alternative – being lean.

Remember that your purpose is to **learn** what form your business is going to take. Sure, you might have decided that you'd like to sell

---

[1]   In fairness, occasionally this will work – but it's a matter of luck and this book is NOT
        about being lucky.
[2]   The other reason is lack of cashflow. We'll cover that later.

handmade soaps but that still leaves many, many questions unanswered – a lean startup finds out those answers as quickly as possible and at the lowest achievable cost.

In practice, this means producing very small batches and putting them in front of your customers. These prototypes need to be in packaging that is as authentic as possible – everything about them that might influence the opinions of your test customers needs to be as near to a final, mass-produced, version as possible.

Doing it this way, you may make no profit at all from your prototypes. Making small batches means you can't buy supplies in bulk (except those that are common across all products of your type). You may have to print labels on your laser printer and pay a designer to come up with a packaging design for what is a very small run.

So, you put your prototypes in front of your test customers, at a price that would mean you'd make a profit once you produced in greater quantities. Did they buy? What was their reaction to the product? Would they have preferred a different scent, flavour, style of packaging, label, size, weight etc? Get specific feedback and remain open-minded. Listen carefully to what they're saying and how they're reacting. The only thing I can promise is that you'll be surprised – it may be a big surprise or a little one – but these surprises are worth real money.

So, you take the feedback and create a new prototype. Rinse and repeat until you hit the sweet spot – the point at which customers readily buy what you have to offer at the price you want to set.

How many cycles of prototyping should I expect?
It's impossible to be exact but I'd be surprised if you could get away with fewer than three. I suggest that if you get it right first time, you're either underpricing (in which case, run another trial at a higher price) or not truly listening to your customers. If the process drags on cycle after cycle, perhaps the product is fundamentally wrong (this is very rare) and you should be listening to your customers to find out what they would like.

Where should I test my prototypes?

For most craft businesses, the best place to test is in front of real customers. You could, for example, hire a table at a local school fete or small craft fair. Make it a small table and don't take too much stock – enough to test however many products you wish to prototype. Try to test each round at similar events so that you can be sure your results are due to the changes you've made to your products and not because the first round was at a jumble sale and the second at a major craft fair.

Remember that the point of the day is not to make money but to improve your products. The acid test is whether people buy at the price you've set, not to make a big profit that day. Profit comes later when you ratchet up production of your fully developed product.

Even if you intend to sell primarily online, you should get some initial feedback face to face. Once that's done, you can prototype using a basic online shop.

Isn't this expensive and time-consuming?

No – because what you end up with is a product that you know will sell. You can then go ahead and crank up production, securing the lowest possible material costs because you're buying in bulk.

Let's use a candle maker as an example. She's discovered, through her prototyping, that people really like aromatherapy themed candles. Her original prototypes were fruit scented but, by listening to customers, she learned that they were most excited by the idea of a warm bath with a revitalising luxury candle. So a "revitalise" branded candle created from a mix of scents was more appealing than the "zesty lemon" our candle-maker had originally planned.

Had she gone with her lemon candle, she would have produced in bulk (in order to make a profit) and might have achieved modest sales – anything more successful would have been a matter of pure luck.

Having spent a little time and money on prototyping, she discovered that her audience likes candles that are labelled by their intended purpose rather than their main ingredient. So she can now safely make these candles in bulk knowing that there's a market for the product. Once she has her "revitalise" candle up and running, she can then prototype "relaxing" or "soothing" alternatives. The process would be similar, except that she'd probably only need a couple of attempts before hitting on the right recipe.

It's the difference between guessing what will sell and knowing what will sell.

Case Study: MakingYourOwnCandles

In 2009, we wanted to find out whether the market for candle making kits was big enough to support a potentially full time business. I had used various techniques to find out what the levels of internet traffic were likely to be (MYOC was intended as a solely online business) but this was all theory until we put our products in front of our customers.

We developed three prototype kits in several variations because we needed our shop to have a credible number of products. However, each of these kits was similar and we used the same components across each. We bought boxes in small quantities, printed labels and instruction leaflets using an inkjet, used standard Royal Mail delivery rather than cheaper alternatives. All in all, our profit on each item was modest. But, the aim of the exercise was to answer the following questions:

1.   Could this be a worthwhile business?

2.   What kits did customers want enough to buy?

The answer to question 1 came in the form of turnover and traffic. As for the products themselves, they changed substantially as a result both of customer feedback and our experiences of creating and fulfilling them.

Once their format was settled, we were able to increase how much money we made per item whilst also improving their presentation through professional labels, printed leaflets and better boxes. Because we took the time to experiment with the products, they've remained popular and very profitable ever since. And each new product is introduced in the same way – as an experiment.

WHAT ARE YOU GOING TO MAKE?

We've covered how to use prototypes to come up with your final product, but how do you decide what to sell?

That final word is critical – these are products to **sell**. The purpose of prototyping is to find out exactly what people will pay for but you need to begin somewhere. What craft will you choose? What aspect of that craft?

First I want to introduce two key principles of making money from a craft business: *the two Ps*.

THE FIRST P: PREMIUM

This is possibly the most important piece of advice in this entire book. I strongly recommend that you do **not** compete on price at the bottom end of the market. You should make products at the mid-market and, preferably, premium end of the price range.

There are two reasons why I recommend this approach:

Competition/Expectation

Competing on price is a mug's game - Tesco, Wilkinson and Matalan will always be able to beat you. For example, their candles are made in the thousands by machines. Wax is poured robotically into moulds, holes are drilled down the middle and a pre-waxed wick added after the candle has set. It's often the wrong wick, leading to "tunneling"[1], with poor quality wax, which causes smoking. In other words, the candle looks ok – until you come to use it.

As a crafter, you do not want to be associated with poor quality, cheap products. By creating a premium product, your competition becomes other suppliers of high-priced items rather than the local supermarket – this is a good place to be.

Another example. Let's say you make children's dressing up costumes. Now, I could pop into Asda and pick up a pumpkin costume for a fiver. My expectation is that it'll be rubbish – mainly because of the price but

---

[1]   Where the flame isn't strong enough to melt all the wax, causing it to form a tunnel as it burns and ultimately drowning.

also because of where I bought it. If I want to treat my son, on the other hand, I might look on eBay. If I see your hand-made costume listed at £6, my mind files it alongside the products from Asda and Wilkinson and I scroll down to look at other choices. If the costume is, say, £17.50, then I'm more likely to at least click on the listing and see what there is about it that makes it worth the extra. You're in the running for my business.

Oh, and by the way, you're probably thinking the £17.50 for a custom costume doesn't sound very "premium" but it's all relative. In a market where the bottom end is around the £5 mark, charging 3x as much makes it premium.

Margin

Margin is, essentially, the percentage difference between the cost of making a product and the price the customer pays. If a bar of soap costs £2 to make and you sell it for £4, that's a 100% margin[1] and a gross profit of £2. A premium bar of hand made soap might cost, say, £6. In order to make it a "premium" product you might have to use more expensive (for example organic) ingredients which might push the cost up to £2.50 for example. Your margin is now 143%[2] and the gross profit per unit has gone from £2 to £3.50.

And before you say "yes, but I'll sell fewer of them" don't be so sure! Over the years, I've run dozens of experiments across multiple industries and I can tell you that, in almost every case, profits go up when you increase the price. In many cases, the number of units sold also goes up.

Why? Because people associate value with price. If you're a silversmith selling jewellery at a craft fair, customers will assume that an item you mark up at £25 has more value than one marked £10, even if they're very similar.

This isn't about fooling people or ripping them off. It's about matching quality and expectations. I would expect a £25 pillar candle to be of noticeably higher quality, using better, more expensive ingredients and packaged better (of which more later) than a £10 candle. My point

---

[1] There are many types of margin – but let's not muddy the water at this point
[2] $((£6-£2.50)/£2.50) \times 100$

is that the candle maker could have priced that candle at £15 and I, as a customer, would have found reasons to justify that price also. In the end, as a customer, I must be satisfied that I got value. Value is not the same as cheapest!

Please, as a final note, don't under-price out of a lack of confidence in your own ability. Customers will either buy your product or they won't – but, in my view, you should at least give them the chance to buy a premium version and if you find yourself competing on price, try another product or you will end up resenting the amount of work you have to put into the business for very little return

THE SECOND P: PERSONALISATION

People like to make and buy craft items because they're the polar opposite of the generic, mass produced products that make up such a large part of our day to day existence. By their nature, each hand-made product is, to a greater or lesser extent, unique.

However, deliberate personalisation is also an extremely effective way to increase sales. For some crafts this is easy enough, you may be considering it already. But a degree of personalisation is possible for most crafts.

This doesn't necessarily mean making the product specifically for one person. Whilst it might well be possible to create a profitable business making knitted dog coats with the name of the dog sewn in (or, for a lower cost of production, sewn on), any way in which you can make the product more personal will increase its attractiveness.

Let's return to our silversmith. One of her staple products might be charm bracelets. To increase the personalisation of these bracelets, she could create a range that includes, amongst the charms, the customer's birth stone. This could either be done to order, or, with a little forethought, added at the point of purchase.

Personalisation can be used both to increase the number of items you sell as well as increasing the price you can charge.

Case Study: Say it with Brownies
www.sayitwithbrownies.co.uk

Anita hand-bakes batches of gorgeous brownies to order. Customers can specify one of a range of stickers to be attached to the very attractive packaging with a message such as "thank you" or "get well soon". Anita will also add a hand written tag to each order.

This level of personalisation makes this product a perfect gift. Let's face it, most of us would prefer a box of brownies over a bunch of flowers wouldn't we?

Say it with brownies is backed up with a professionally designed website which, along with the packaging, projects the sort of image that makes it possible to charge good value, but premium, prices.

MILESTONE 1: PICK YOUR PRODUCT

Right, it's time to make your first decision. Which craft market are you going to choose? I suggest you pick as wide a market as possible and allow your research to direct you to the most profitable specific products.

Example markets:

candle making

soap making

confectionary

preserve making

clothing and costumes

jewellery

metal work

basket making

funiture maker

card making

beadwork

leatherwork

model making

needlework – crocheting, cross-stitch, embroidery, knitting, lace, needlepoint, sewing picture framing

decorative crafts

ceramics

painting

toymaking

weaving

stained glass

woodwork

...and that's just a partial list.

RULE NUMBER 1: DO WHAT YOU LOVE

It makes sense to pick a craft you already know and love. It might well be that, as a result of your research, you might end up serving a slightly different part of the market than you expect at first but you're going to be spending a lot of time building your craft business, you might as well enjoy it!

For example, Peta and I love candle making but we don't sell candles. Our research indicated that the market for candle making kits suited us better.

However, don't make the mistake of believing that just because you love to make a particular craft item, other people will be happy to pay for them. That's the purpose of market research.

MARKET RESEARCH

Online

The best place to start is usually online. The chances are that someone, somewhere is already selling into your chosen market. Do a search on your craft name and see who crops up.

For example, if you Google "hand made soap", you'll see a page full of ads, photos and website addresses. Go through each of the main sites looking for the following:

- Are they professionally presented?

- Do they feature premium products?

- What are the prevailing prices?

- What is the difference between the lower priced items and those at the premium end?

- Are the online retailers long established?

It's a good idea to make notes as you go.

Your first reaction, if you see a lot of companies and individuals operating in your craft might be to panic. However, I'd be a lot more worried if next to no-one was in the market. Competition means that there is a worthwhile market there – whether that's entirely online or, as is more often the case, an online store or simple website that supports a physical business.

You also shouldn't feel the need to find a gap in the market, especially if you intend to sell mainly at craft fairs. Unless you're unlucky enough to find someone else very close to you who is doing exactly what you intend to do, your gap in the market is your locality.

If someone is already operating in your local market, then take the opportunity to look at their business and see how they're doing – you might be able to learn a lot! This isn't about stealing ideas from other people, not at all – it's about learning what you can from them and seeing how you can apply this to your business.

Case Study: MakingYourOwnCandles.co.uk

Since we started, and probably largely because of the fact that the business is featured in my book "How to set up an online business", a number of copy-cat candle kit retailers have set themselves up.

In each and every case, they have looked at our website and attempted to copy our kits or, in one famous case, rip off everything including kit contents, instructions and even ecommerce provider[1].

Whilst this might seem like a quick route to setting up a business, it's actually just a shortcut to insolvency. You see, the website or craft stall that customers see is just the tip of the iceberg, the important stuff is what goes on behind it. Our website is like the "face" of the company – it looks as it does because of what we believe in and how we run our business. You can't expect to simply steal our face, plop it onto another body and expect it to act like MakingYourOwnCandles.

Every single one of these copycats closed down having lost a lot of money.

Looking at how other people do it is important (not least because often what you learn is how not to do it) but you must then apply what you've learned to your own business. You might like their product pictures, for example. So, you'd work out what it was you liked about them (perhaps the lighting or the fact that they're shot against a white background) and apply that to your product photos. You shouldn't, on the other hand, decide you're going to make a rip-off of their soap because the photo looked nice!

---

[1] This particular miscreant received a "fruity" communication from us

Finally, don't make the mistake of assuming that just because a website exists, the company or people behind it are successful. Many aren't – it's just as useful for you to spot the mistakes they make (for example, if you find the ordering process frustrating) as it is to note down the things they do well.

Craft fairs

Whether or not you intend to sell at craft fairs, you should make it your business to go to plenty. This is partly because your customers will be there and you'll be able to familiarise yourself with the level of quality they expect to see, as well as the prices they typically pay.

It's also because you'll get an idea of the range of crafts and how the stall holders lay out their products. Pay special attention to labelling and packaging. Think about how you would see their products as a customer – do they look like they're of premium quality? How are crafters offering personalisation? Which ones look successful?

If you're paying proper attention, you'll be able to separate the regular craft attendees from the newcomers. The regulars are worth examining closely, and talking to if you have the confidence. They would not be turning up week in week out (and often across the country) if they weren't making money. What is it about their product and its presentation that means they're a success?

Craft fairs are a gold mine – and if you look closely at the products on offer, particularly those in your chosen field, you'll probably feel better about your own abilities. It's rare indeed that I've seen a candle I couldn't imagine making myself.

Craft Retailers

Hobbycraft is a good place to go to see the retail side of crafting. Craft retailers like Hobbycraft don't sell completed crafts, they sell kits and materials.

Is there something in that for you? Have you thought about supplying materials to crafters rather than the finished goods? The size of retailers such as Hobbycraft and the craft sections in many mainstream retailers suggests there's a big market for it. This, after all, is exactly what we did with MakingYourOwnCandles.

Craft Stockists

On the other hand, many retailers stock craft items (some, such as John Lewis have craft items *and* materials). Take a look at the mid to upper range offerings to see what your customers expect in terms of quality and price.

Case Study: Jo Malone

Perfumier Jo Malone has a range of scented candles (google "jo malone candles" and you'll find them).

They have two ranges. Their "home" candles retail for around £40 for a 200g candle (approximately whiskey tumbler size). Now, I'd call that premium.

But their "luxury" range trumps that. Here's the blurb from one of them:

"The ultimate home accessory. The luxury candle will infuse the compelling scent of Lime Basil & Mandarin throughout your rooms. Burn time 230 hours. Complimentary Jo Malone™ matches included."

How much do you think this 2.5KG candle retails for? I'll leave you to find out. Suffice it to say, I've had holidays that have cost less.

So, if you're ever in doubt about the value of what you do and whether people are prepared to pay for it, just remember Jo Malone and similar retailers.

MILESTONE 2: MAKE YOUR PLANS

You should now have one or more (more is better) ideas of the sorts of products you'd like to create and sell.

It's now time to get specific. You now need to make a plan to get from this stage to having products ready for sale. For now, we're concentrating on getting the product right – rather than worrying too much about how we're going to promote or distribute it. You do need to think about pricing at this stage (the next chapter covers this in depth) but only at a fairly broad level. If, through prototyping, you end up with a product people really like, the price can be set later. It's enough to know, at this point, the general, finger in the air, range.

For example. If I were starting a candle making business today, I'd target the market for decorative pillar candles that make lovely mantelpiece decorations, and the luxury container candle market. I would aim to create candles in the £15-£30 price range and that's specific enough to allow me to experiment with my prototypes without getting bogged down in pence. It's much easier to adapt a popular product to the pockets of its target audience than it is to design to a price from the beginning.

Create a plan with the following headings **for each product**.

Product name

Initial Product Concept

Broad price range

Cycle 1

Ingredients/materials

Instructions for creating one item

Time required to create each item

Date/place for prototype

Feedback

Change list

Cycle 2

Ingredients/materials

Instructions for creating one item

Time required to create each item

Date/place for prototype

Feedback

Change list

Repeat until you have the final product.

Congratulations – finding the right product is the single most difficult part of starting up your own business. Now that you have a product you can be confident in, it's just a question of pricing it properly, making it as cheaply as possible, marketing it effectively and fulfilling all those orders.

Case Study: Say it with Brownies (www.sayitwithbrownies.co.uk)

How did you decide which products to make and sell?

> *"I loved baking so that was a natural choice for me. When I initially decided to create a mail order cake business, I wasn't sure exactly what I was going to make and sell. Originally I was going to bake a variety of goodies including flapjacks, cookies and cakes. However the more I thought about the practicalities of everything, the more I decided to keep my life simple and stick to one thing.*
>
> *Then I came up with the Say It With Brownies name which seemed to work as a play on words, and that kind of made my decision! Brownies are a good option for mail order as they can be tightly wrapped up for the post and I've never had a problem with them being crushed or damaged. They stay fresh for over a week. And most importantly, of all of the cakes that I used to make my friends and colleagues, my brownies were everybody's favourites so I knew I was on to a winner! I played around with different flavours for a few months, and simply chose my favourite six ideas to go onto the menu."*

Case Study: Littlecote Soap Co (www.littlecotesoap.co.uk)

How did you decide which products to make and sell?

> *"I started off with just soaps and bath bombs, I then added bath salts, and as the company grew I added different products and the ranges grew. With toiletries there are some main scent groups and colours so I concentrated on these; Citrus (yellow), Seaweed (Blue), Gardener's/Herbal (Green), Rose (pink).*
>
> *I produced lots of different scents to start with and it soon became clear which were the favourite fragrances. Once I knew which were the best sellers, we then expanded these ranges to include larger*

sizes of the product, mini tester/sampler sizes and other items of the same scent such as lip balms and candles etc.

Sometimes it was very interesting to sell the same product, but labelled with two different names, at the opposite end of the stall to see which sold the best. We listened to customer suggestions, and gave out lots of samples and leaflets."

Chapter 4: Setting a price

You remember that email I sent out to the customers of MakingYourOwnCandles.co.uk asking them to let me know what they wanted to learn about setting up a craft business? Guess what the top response was? Yep, variations of "How do I know what price to charge?". In fact, pricing was mentioned twice as often as the next most popular topic so I've dedicated a whole chapter to it.

HOW MUCH?

Inside most of us lurks an insecurity. We imagine ourselves at our first craft fair, the fruits of our labours laid out on the table. Up sidles a likely looking customer. She picks up one of our products, rotates it in her hand and sniffs it (I'm imagining a candle but substitute any craft you like here). She makes an approving noise and shows it to her friend who turns the candle over to find the price sticker. Her face creases into a rictus of mixed incredulity and derision. "How much? Are you mad?" She says, and storms off to be rude to the next stall-holder.

Sound familiar? If we were asked to explain why pricing is such a problem issue for us, we'd probably say it was because of sound business reasons – getting the price right is essential for profitability. However, for many of us, the real motivator is our underlying fear that someone will tell us, in so many words, that our craft skills don't match the price we want to charge.

Well, that's the elephant in the room exposed. It's time to get over it. Firstly, whilst it's possible that some customers looking at your products will think they're overpriced, they're unlikely to say so out loud. Secondly, if a customer does mention price, it's probably a negotiating tactic. They're acknowledging that they like the product enough to buy it, they just don't want to pay the ticket price. Thirdly, don't assume you can read the minds of people – some will simply be unable to afford your product so what you see as disdain may actually be disappointment.

If you've done your research so far, you know what sort of quality is on offer at what sort of price. You therefore know that your products are of at least this level of quality. So relax – you really are good enough!

I'm not going to pretend that setting the right price for your products is straightforward or easy. You need to see it as a fluid process, not something that you decide up front and then never change. You might also set different prices for the same products if they're sold in several marketplaces – your craft fair, eBay, website and retail prices would usually be different to each other.

I suggest you take the same attitude to pricing that you do to other aspects of your business, including prototyping. Your aim is to find the optimum price range and then to move the actual price within that as you run promotions or sell through other platforms. As with prototyping, you will find a sweet spot where the price you set generates the maximum income.

COST

Cost is different to price. The cost of a product is how much you have to pay to create it. The price is what a customer pays.

All pricing begins with working out the cost to you. I don't know whether you watch programmes such as "The Hotel Inspector" but one of the most common complaints Alex Polizzi has when she visits failing hotels is that they don't know the cost of providing their service – even to the extent that they can't tell her whether they make a profit on their breakfast.

In the case of craft products, the most obvious component is the cost of materials. So, the first thing to do is to take the recipe you settled on after prototyping and work out how much each item would cost to make.

Economies of scale

To work out the per-item cost, you must first decide how many you're going to make. Remember, that, as a result of your research, you can be pretty certain that your product is going to be popular (as long as you price it correctly). My advice is to look at the quantity discounts from your suppliers and work out which level of discount you want to aim for.

For example, let's look at another aromatherapy example - soap this time. We can buy organic soap bases in these quantities at these prices:

1kg   £5

5kg   £24

11.5kg   £50

23kg   £90

Our recipe calls for 100g of base per soap. So (ignoring wastage etc for simplicity's sake), we can make 10 soaps per kg. If we buy the smallest quantity of base, this means the cost per soap is £5/10 soaps = 50p per soap. On the other hand, the biggest quantity is enough for 230 soaps at a cost per soap of £90/230 = 39p per soap.

There are two things to consider in this case. Firstly, given that the cost of the produced soap is likely to be at least £5, the 11p saving on buying the biggest quantity probably wouldn't normally be worth it. However, that base is probably going to be used in all your soaps so it wouldn't go to waste.

If it were me, I would probably order the 11.5kg block which would be enough to make 115 soaps in a number of flavours and offer a cost saving of around 7p per soap.

So, you need to think about how much you are willing to invest in stock – the more you make, the cheaper each product will be but the higher the amount of cash you're tying up.

Apply the same process to each ingredient. We use a spreadsheet to make this easier (and less open to a mistake).

Packaging and labelling
Much the same applies to your packaging and labelling. We'll cover these in more detail later but, essentially, the more you order, the cheaper it will be. This applies whether you're using plain generic boxes or having them custom printed, laser printed label sheets or those from a professional print house.

The trick, again, is to order enough to satisfy reasonable demand and achieve some sort of economies of scale, without lumbering yourself with too much packaging that may go out of date before it's used.

Your time

At this stage, you shouldn't usually include the cost of your time in the calculation. Normally, you'd be recommended to do this to arrive at the true cost of your product but this only applies if you could otherwise have spent the same time doing something else that could have earned money.

When we set up MakingYourOwnCandles, one of its purposes was provide a source of income for Peta so that she didn't have to find part time work when our son started at school. In that case, the choice was between making candle kits or working on a checkout at Budgens so it would make sense to include a labour cost since she would otherwise have been earning a wage. If it takes 15 minutes to put a kit together then the labour cost needs to be £1.50 (approximately the national minimum wage for 15 minute's work).

If the time you're using is your spare time, though, there is no need to include a labour charge. Later on, you might reduce your current job's hours to spend more time on your business – and at that point you must reflect the labour cost in your products.

The costs of doing business

For each product, you should add its proportion of the fixed costs of your business. Let's say you have an eBay shop, for example, which costs you £20 per month. You expect to sell 100 products per month so the cost of the shop per product is 20p.

In our case, our main additional cost is marketing. We attract business largely through Google AdWords (the ads you see when you do a Google search). So, we divide the monthly budget for this by the number of products sold per month. If we sell 200 products a month, for example, and our AdWords bill is £300 then we know that, on average, the cost of marketing was around £1.50 per product.

This approach works well if your products are all around the same price but if they vary a lot, it's probably fairer to work out what percentage of your turnover your marketing budget represents and apply that to each product. But in that case, you must use the selling price (since turnover is the total cash you take in, not related to cost price).

At this stage, stick to using your marketing budget and dividing it by anticipated sales.

Do your best to account for all additional costs – including subscriptions, book-keeping costs etc, to get an accurate figure.

VAT

If you intend to charge VAT[1] then remember that if you and your supplier are both VAT registered (they usually are) you can reclaim the VAT you pay when you buy your materials, reducing the net cost of them to you. So, before you add the 20% on top of your cost price, make sure all the prices of your materials are shown excluding VAT

Is your brain hurting yet? Mine is.

Here are a couple of examples which should hopefully make the process clear.

Candle Maker #1

Ruth is starting to make candles – she's doing it purely as an additional income and is not registering for VAT. She intends to sell them at a craft-fair at the end of the month. She's chosen to make candles in vintage tea-cups which she buys in charity shops.

As she's very sensible, she's purchased our bulk container candle kit which makes 40 tea cup candles at a cost (at the time of writing) of around £75 including three different candle making scents and three dyes.

She's decided, then, to make 40 candles to sell at the craft-fair.

Cost per candle

[1]   We'll cover whether you should register later.

Materials

Tea cup (average)	£1.00
Wax, wick, dye, scent etc	£1.85

Labelling

Brown suitcase tags	£0.10

Time

Not charged	£0.00

Cost of doing business

Craft-fair fee	£0.50 (the £20 fee divided by 40 candles)

TOTAL   **£3.45 per candle**

One important note: this cost per candle assumes she will sell all of them. She visited the craft-fair when it was last on and, based on the number of people they expect, she thinks this is a reasonable target. Had it been a smaller event, she could have made 20, although the cost per candle would then have been higher.

Candle Maker #2

Liz has been making candles for some time and runs it as a part time business. She's registered for VAT. She's also going to the same craft-fair and has also decided to make 40 tea-cup candles.

Cost per candle

Materials

Tea cup (average)	£1.00[1]
Wax, wick, dye, scent etc	£1.54[2]

Labelling

Brown suitcase tags	£0.08

Time

5 minutes per candle	£0.50

Cost of doing business

Craft-fair fee net of VAT)	£0.42 (the £20 fee divided by 40 candles

TOTAL   **£3.54 per candle**

---

[1]   Charity shops don't charge VAT so we show the price paid for the cup, not the net figure
[2]   The cost of the materials net of VAT (since we can reclaim it)

WORK OUT THE VALUE OF A SALE

Not all sales are equal, and you need to bear this in mind before you set your prices. For example, it is usually far, far, cheaper to sell to an existing customer than to find a new one. This is most obvious if you intend to sell online. Unless you have been recommended, new customers will usually find you by some sort of marketing – in our case Google AdWords. Let's say our average sale is £20 and the average AdWords cost of achieving that first sale is £5 (neither of these figures is the true amount, but they serve as an illustration) then the income net of marketing is £15. If that customer comes directly to us next time, we've effectively saved £5 on that second purchase because we didn't need to advertise to them.

Similarly, if a customer buys their first product from you at a craft-fair, takes away your business card and then buys from your eBay shop, again the cost of that second purchase is much lower.

We'll talk later about the critical issue of encouraging repeat purchases through marketing and customer service but it's worth thinking about this when you're pricing – in other words, can you offer different pricing for new customers compared with existing customers?

Could you develop products that encourage repeat purchases? For example, a limited edition collection? Refills so customers can make more craft items from your kits at a reduced price?

PRICING

There are three commonly used techniques for pricing and it's likely you'll use all three.

PRICING TECHNIQUE 1: MARGIN

You now have your cost price. This sets the lower limit below which you must never sell your products if you want to make a profit. Bear in mind that the approach is the same whether you are selling direct to the public, as will be the usual case, or to a retailer or other third party for them to sell. The only difference is that if they're prepared to buy in bulk, you can reduce your margin per product whilst still making much more money overall.

The amateur way to price goods is to take the cost price of the materials and add a profit margin. Traditionally, for craft products, the margin is 100% - in other words, you take the cost and double it to get your selling price. However, the "cost" here is just the material cost and the 100% margin is just a guesstimate to take into account all the other factors that need to be added. In other words, if you look back at the examples earlier, if Ruth was using the "cost + 100%" approach, she'd be using £2.85 (the cost of the tea cup + the cost of the wax, scent, wick and dye) as her "cost" price rather than the much more accurate and businesslike true figure of £3.45. She'd therefore set her selling price at £5.70 (or, more sensibly, £5.99) – or £2.85 + 100%.

"Materials Cost + 100%" is "finger in the air" business at its worst and, not surprisingly, I don't recommend you use it.

It's much better to start with the more accurate cost figure you've worked out and add a reasonable profit to it – 75% for example.

In that case, Ruth would sell her candles for £5.99 which is a few pence less than £3.45 + 75%.[1]

Hold the phone! That's exactly the same as she'd charge using the other method! Yes, but the difference here is that the "cost + 100%"

---

[1]   Some people struggle with percentages but that's what calculators are for! In this case, using the Windows Calculator, you'd type "3.45 + 75" and hit the % then = buttons. This should show £6.0375 which we'll round down to £5.99

version is a guess whereas using accurate cost figures and a lower percentage is much more certain. What if the craft fair cost £50? Using our method, this would be accounted for in the true cost price, using the "finger in the air" method it would not. We would make the same 75% profit irrespective, whereas with the other method your actual profit will vary (to the point of disappearing in some extreme cases).

I appreciate that "materials cost + 100%" seems simple and takes away the decision about what mark-up to use. However, this simplicity comes at the price of you not being entirely sure how much you're actually making for each product.

If you use our more accurate figure, which includes every aspect of the cost price, not just the materials, and then add a consistent margin, you will achieve the same profit levels from every product.

If it helps at all, I think that 75% - 150% is a good profit margin so "true cost + 75-150%" is a reasonable place to begin.

Okay, so Ruth has set her price at £5.99.

VAT

Liz (the other candle maker in our example), on the other hand, is registered for VAT so what does she do? If we use the same approach, we get £6.20 as the selling price - £3.54 (the cost price net of VAT)+ 75%.

However, her price must include VAT so she's actually only receiving £5.16 net (£6.20 – the VAT) which means she's earning a total of £1.62 net profit per candle whereas Ruth is making the princely sum of £2.54 net profit.

Actually, it's not quite as bad as that – don't forget that, in the cost price of the candle, we included 50p which represents Liz's labour cost. So Liz actually makes £2.12 per candle.

(I think I need a lie down.)

If Liz wants to make the same profit as Ruth, she must increase her price per candle to around £6.79.

This neatly illustrates the disadvantage of registering for VAT – if you are competing with other businesses and selling to the public, then you are at a small price disadvantage.

SHOULD YOU REGISTER FOR VAT?

You must register for VAT if you expect your turnover over the next 12 months to be more than the VAT threshold (£77,000 in 2012). I suggest this is likely to be rare if you're just starting up but it's worth remembering as you grow your business.

You can also voluntarily register for VAT whatever your expected turnover. This will allow you to reclaim the VAT on things you buy for the business (as long as it included VAT, of course).

Broadly speaking, you should consider registering if you expect to sell your products to businesses that are themselves VAT registered. These businesses can reclaim the VAT so they don't, in effect, pay the extra 20%. You, as a VAT registered business, are then able to reclaim the VAT you pay on materials etc, reducing the cost of creating your product.

If your business is below the threshold and you're selling **direct to consumers**, there's much less of a case to register, at least to begin with. There's no doubt that being VAT registered increases your credibility as a company but that's not usually worth more than the price advantage a non-VAT company gets by being able to undercut your VAT registered competition.

PRICING TECHNIQUE 2: COMPETITION

It's important to work out your margin-based price **before** you look at what your competitors charge. This is because if you do it the other way round, you will always be influenced by their figures rather than settling on a margin you'd be happy with.

When it comes to looking at your competitors, make sure that you're comparing like with like. For example, if you're making silver jewellery for sale at a craft-fair, you should ideally be checking to see what other silversmiths charge at fairs rather than their online price. Having said that, if they're selling an almost identical product for half your intended selling price then this would require investigation to find out how they can produce it so cheaply.

The beauty of crafts is the fact that they vary so much. If you sold a specific brand of Hawaiian Ukuleles, for example, customers can very easily check online to see how your price compares. With hand-made soap, on the other hand, whilst customers will have a range they'll consider reasonable, it's pretty wide. An organic bar containing specialist ingredients will retail for more than a more standard bar and it's unlikely the prospective customer will find anything identical to compare it with.

One thing to beware. Don't assume, just because you find a shop online that sells a similar product to yours at a very different price, that this means they're making a profit. Not everyone is going to have worked out their prices as methodically as you – many of these online traders will be selling lots of products but at too low a price to make a reasonable income. Equally, they might be charging too much and not selling very many.

So, by all means, check that your price fits within a reasonable range by looking at competitors but, unless you have very good reason, your actual price should be set using the true cost + margin method.

If you find, on visiting a craft-fair, that there are a number of other crafters selling a similar product and the price they charge is similar to or less than your intended price, then this is good news. Why? Because it strongly suggests there's a decent market for your product – but you might need to find a new angle to differentiate your creation. This

Unique Selling Point (USP) should be clear enough to clearly separate you into a category of your own in the minds of customers, and this allows you to set the price you want.

Examples include going organic, using natural ingredients, personalising, limited editions, collection pieces etc.

Exactly the same applies to whatever marketplace you use – whether it's your own website, or a platform such as eBay, Folksy or Amazon. Just make sure you're making a fair comparison.

In the cases of Ruth and Liz, by visiting their craft-fair, they can see that teacup candles of the quality they're offering are selling for between £5.99 and £7.99 so they're pricing looks fine. If they'd found that the range was lower, they could consider using Soy container wax and organic scents so that they could charge a premium.

PRICING TECHNIQUE 3: EXPERIMENTATION

Pricing techniques 1 and 2 have set your retail price based on margin and competition. However, in the end, every product is only worth what a customer is prepared to pay – bearing in mind that the perceived value of a product is strongly influenced by its ticket price.

You should not consider this retail price as a fixed, immovable number – rather it's a starting point. You are seeking the sweet spot – the price that allows you to make the most overall profit. It doesn't necessarily follow that if you reduce the retail price, more people will buy a product (because they will see it as worth less). However, it does follow that if you offer a promotional price below the retail figure you will almost always see an increase in buyers. The key issue is whether the increase in sales compensates for the drop in profit per item.

Pricing should not be decided in a panic – in other words, you shouldn't suddenly discount your stock if sales haven't been up to much during the first couple of hours of your craft-fair. This is especially the case if you're using the craft-fair to prototype – remember the purpose is to firm up your product and its pricing, if you sell it for next to nothing, you've learned next to nothing.

A more organised approach is to vary pricing in a structured fashion. In the case of a craft-fair, this might be to use the full price in the morning (keeping careful note of sales) and then running a promotion in the afternoon showing the original price and, say, a 10% discount. You will probably sell more in the afternoon and, if you keep proper records, you'll be able to tell whether your earnings were better before the promotion started (when you had a higher margin on each product) or after (when you sold more). At the end of the day, the key figure is how much net profit did you make – which technique worked best?

PRICING STRATEGIES

Once you've settled on your retail price, using the margin, competition and experimentation methods, you can then use various pricing strategies to get the most out of your potential sales.

Discount Promotions

Everyone likes a discount! Make sure you set a definite end date and restore the original price at the end. At MakingYourOwnCandles, we've found that 20% is the most effective discount – encouraging extra sales without decimating the profitability of each product.

Stock-clearances

If you're going to stop making a particular product, slash the price to get the stock cleared. A good example is post Christmas sales of festive products.

Loyalty discounts

Remember, repeat customers cost you less to sell to, so you can afford to incentivise them to buy from you again. At MakingYourOwnCandles we apply an automatic 5% discount for every order our customers make after their second. They don't need to remember – the discount shows on their order as soon as they place it.

Discounts for larger orders

Because your fixed costs remain the same, the larger the order a customer makes, the greater your profit on it. You can pass some of that extra profit back to the customer in the form of a lower price to encourage more people to buy in bulk. In our case, we sell kits for making 20 or 40 container candles – these are our two best selling products (in revenue and profit terms) because they represent great value.

BOGOF etc

Craft products have a significant cost price and, if you're operating on a true cost price + 75% model, offering a Buy One Get One Free promotion is likely to wipe you out. However, variations on this such as "Buy Three Get One Free" or, put another way, "Buy four, pay for three" can be very popular – everyone wants to get something for nothing

Free delivery

Take care with this – it might be worth a try if you're selling online but you might eat significantly into your profit margin by making delivery free (unless your product allows postage to be very cheap). In our experience at least, free delivery no longer impresses customers, they would prefer a percentage discount.

There's almost no limit to the types of promotional schemes you can come up with – feel free to experiment once you feel comfortable with your business, product range and, most importantly, customers.

Case Study: Littlecote Soap Co (www.littlecotesoap.co.uk)

Elaine carefully works out the true cost price including labelling, packaging and labour and then applies a 100% mark-up when selling to the trade or a shop. Where she's selling direct to the public, she applies a 300% mark-up on the cost price. Soap making is a great example of where a high-value product can be made from ingredients that are relatively low-priced – however, "cosmetic crafts" can be relatively expensive to set up in the first place because of regulatory requirements.

MILESTONE 3: SET YOUR BASE RETAIL PRICE

Pricing may sometimes feel more art than science but it really isn't. It's about working out how much the product costs to make then setting a profitable retail price based on that plus a margin – making sure that it fits with the competition.

Once you have that in your back pocket, you can experiment with varying the pricing through promotional discounts of one sort or another. Just stay organised and write everything down so you know what works and what doesn't.

CHAPTER 5: THE POWER OF PREMIUM

Competing on price at the bottom end of the market is a game for mugs and robots. As a crafter, your creations deserve to be pitched at the mid to premium buyer so that you get the reward you deserve. Slap a low price ticket on your willow-weave basket and potential customers will see a cheap cane creation like the one they saw in Wilkinsons. Give it the price it deserves and many will be compelled to pick it up and look closer to see what makes it so much more valuable than they're used to.

Bear in mind that "premium" is a relative term – in some markets the actual price will still be quite low but your product will be at the upper end of the range. Quality hand-made soaps, for example, go for £6-£9; not exactly a fortune but more than the entry level hand-made soaps which end up being compared with the more expensive of the mass-manufactured brands.

On the other hand, I'm not suggesting you take a leaf out of the Jo Malone book and try selling a 2.5kg candle for £260! They may, or may not, be able to get away with this but you probably can't. By "premium" I mean at the top end of the normal range, not right off the scale.

WHAT MAKES IT PREMIUM?

Imagine, for a moment, that I've placed five pillar candles on a table. They're all the same size and colour. If I told you that I'd bought them from various retailers and crafters, and that they ranged in price from £5 to £25, do you reckon you could put them into exact price order? Probably not.

How about if I told you that one of them cost £25 but all the others were less than £15 – do you think you could spot the £25 candle? I suggest that most people would have a greater success rate if asked to point out the premium product from a group if they know there's only one – although it would be far from 100% accurate.

Now imagine I put the candles back into their packaging (assuming they had any) and replaced them on the table. Do you think you could spot the premium candle now? In fact, I'd bet that you could pretty accurately order them from most expensive to least with very few mistakes.

The point is this. Whilst the *justification* for a premium price might well be the quality of the materials used to make the product, the evidence of a product's premium status is, more often than not, the quality and professionalism of its packaging and presentation.

BE PICKY ABOUT PACKAGING

Customers make judgements about the value of a product based largely on its packaging. That's not to say that you can put any old tat in a nice box and sell it for a fortune. No indeed – the product inside the box must match the expectations the packaging has created in the potential buyer. The point is that if you don't have good packaging then those expectations, and the perceived value of the product inside, will be lower.

Put it this way – take two identical, high quality bars of hand made soap. Shrink-wrap one and stick a Dymo label on it. Put the other in a properly sized box, with a window in the front, nice lettering and containing tissue paper or straw for the soap to sit in. Which one would, on average, make more money for you?

It's true that the packaging for the second bar of soap would be more expensive but this would be more than compensated for the higher price that could be charged and almost certainly higher sales. The only situation in which this would not apply is if you're selling a "job lot" or deliberately presenting the products as packaging-free (a warehouse clearance event for example).

Many of our products, after all, are sold to be given as gifts – the better the presentation, the more valuable the gift will seem in the eyes of the recipient, exactly what our customer wants.

All we're using is the association that most human beings have between high quality packaging and higher price. As long as the quality of the product inside the box is **worthy** of its packaging then all you're doing is giving your creation the best chance to shine, allowing it to put on its poshest frock.

BOXES

Most craft products are best presented in a box and it's possible to get good quality gift boxes in relatively small quantities from online suppliers such as www.boxmart.co.uk. Don't be afraid to look outside the usual gift categories - it might be that, in your case, a standard brown box is more suitable or even a bottle carrier.

Try to find boxes that will suit more than one product in your range – that way you can take advantage of quantity discounts without having to have too many different box sizes tying up cashflow on your shelves.

Just make sure the box is fit for the intended purpose and, if you sell online, work out how you're going to get it to your customers without damage.

There's no need, particularly at the beginning, to have the boxes printed – not least because this can be very expensive and requires you to order in bulk. A much cheaper and more flexible alternative is to use plain boxes and order stickers or sleeves to decorate them.

PAPERWORK

The days of having to print your leaflets, flyers and stickers in their thousands are mercifully in the past. New digital printing techniques mean online printing companies can offer low quantities at reasonable prices. Pop along to www.yourcraftbusiness.co.uk to find out which companies I currently recommend for digital printing.

Alternatively, you can print at least some of your promotional paperwork ("merchandising") from home using your existing printer. However, do bear in mind that inkjet ink is water soluble so if there's the remotest chance of a document getting wet, consider either printing on a laser (laser toner is waterproof) or photocopying it.

The best all-round workhorse for printing in the home is a colour laser printer. Be careful which you choose, however – if there's any likelihood of you ever wanting to use specialist papers (such as adhesive sticker paper) then you should select a "single pass" printer. Lasers use four different toner colours (black, magenta, cyan and yellow) - and a single pass printer will add all four colours in one journey through the print path whereas a multi-pass printer adds one colour at a time. Specialist papers are more likely to jam at the best of times and having them pass four times through the printer path quadruples this chance.

The best value single pass colour laser printer on the market at present is, in my view, the Lexmark C540 (find out more at www.yourcraftbusiness.co.uk) - we have two in almost constant use for leaflet printing, waterslide transfers and general office paperwork. Whilst the toner cartridges are much more expensive than those used by inkjet printers, they have a much higher capacity (typically 1,000 – 2,500 sheets depending on model) and the cost per sheet is much lower.

A decent colour laser printer will be able to print onto die-cut sheets of stickers (only choose those specifically designed for lasers) which you can then peel off. The results are almost indistinguishable from those supplied by an online digital printing firm but they might be more expensive per label so, once you can afford it, it's better to get them professionally printed.

THE ART OF ARTWORK

Are you a print designer? If so, good for you – you can skip to the next section.

If not, do you know someone who is? That is, someone who earns their living creating leaflets, posters or labels for print, not Uncle John whose only qualification is the fact he owns a copy of Microsoft Publisher.

If the answer's "no" to both of these questions, you have two options (neither of which is to go ahead and do it yourself) because the quickest way to undermine the "premium" status of your products is to bodge the packaging design.

The first, and usually best, option is to hire a designer to create your artwork. Personal recommendation is one way to select the right designer but my personal favourite is to use a service such as that offered by 99designs (99designs.co.uk). This is, effectively, a marketplace – you upload your design brief (the website helps you construct this) and set a budget (from £139 for a leaflet design) and designers from around the world will pitch their designs. You only pay for the design you want to keep.

This works beautifully and I've used this a number of times, particularly for logo design. Bear in mind that, once you have a design, you can then modify it to use across multiple products so the cost in the long term is very low.

DIY design

Still not convinced? You're probably a control freak like me and will only be truly happy if you do it all yourself. Well, as long as you're aware of the risks then by all means do so – but you must learn how to do it.

The first step is to get hold of a book called "The Non-Designers Design Book" by Robin Williams (no, not that one). Make sure you get the most recent third edition (there's a link at **www.yourcraftbusiness.co.uk**) This book will decode the mysteries of basic design so that you learn why it isn't cool to centre everything, or to use comic sans – as well as the principles of layout for print.

Once you've done this, you don't then have to create all your graphics from scratch (designers usually don't!). You can use any of the graphics libraries out there (Medialoot.com is a favourite of mine) and, as long as you buy the right licence, modify any downloads to suit.

Labels and similar artwork

For example, suppose you needed a label for your boxed cookies. My favourite site for graphics is en.fotolia.com and searching for "product label" brings up hundreds of possibilities. Usually, you will want to choose "vector" as your image type[1]. For this example, I ended up at this page: http://en.fotolia.com/id/42424816. The vector licence costs four credits (you buy credits using Paypal and, in this case, each credit is £1). Once downloaded, you can use your art package to separate out the label you want to use (you've bought them all so you can use the others later) and modify it by adding your logo and wording.

[1]   Vector graphics are made up of lines and generally look like designed graphics - the alternative type is "bitmap" which is made up of dots. Photos are bitmaps. By choosing vector where possible, your graphics will print nicely at high quality and will scale well if you need them for posters etc.

As for which art package to use, the industry standard is Adobe Illustrator but that's very expensive and overpowered for most of your likely requirements.

Able alternatives are:

DrawPlusX4 *(http://www.serif.com/drawplus/dpx4.aspx)*

British company Serif have a habit of quietly selling previous versions of their software at very low prices. At the time of writing, the latest version is DrawPlusX5 and costs around £80. X4, on the other hand, can be obtained for just £20 or so from the link above. This is excellent value for a product that will do everything you're likely ever to need.

Xara Photo & Graphic Designer MX 2013
(http://www.xara.com/uk/products/designer/)

Xara is another UK company and their Photo & Graphic Designer product combines photo and vector graphic editing in one. At £69.00, it's more expensive than DrawPlusX4 but it offers a wider range of capabilities and is a good choice if you're feeling ambitious

If you're really pushed for cash, Inkscape (http://inkscape.org/) is a free vector editor. It's a little rough around the edges and not as capable as the products from Serif and Xara but it's free! Bear in mind also that it can't handle the .eps format that a lot of downloadable artwork comes in so you'll have to jump through hoops to convert it first before editing. I'd spend the £20, personally, on DrawPlus and use the extra time I don't have to spend monkeying around with graphic conversion on making some products to sell!

Documents

If you need to create a publication that contains more than a couple of pages, then you need to use either a word processor or a desktop publishing application.

You will always get better results using a DTP program for anything other than the most basic layouts. If you want to use a word processor, then stick to very simple layouts. For anything more adventurous, I recommend Serif's PagePlus. Again, if you stick with the last version but one (X5 in this case) you can pick it up for a bargain £20 – go to **http://www.serif.com/pageplus/ppx5.aspx** if you're interested.

Inspiration

If you imagine that designers sit in little cabins the woods smoking whatever designers smoke so that they can come up with unique new designs, think again. Designs are not created in isolation and designers look for inspiration across a whole range of media.

So, don't be afraid to type "jam jar label" into Google's image search (images.google.co.uk) and see what pops up. I'm not, for a moment, suggesting that you rip off someone else's design – for exactly the same reason that you shouldn't rip off someone else's business. Not only is unethical, it's also likely to fail. Your design needs to come from you and be consistent with other aspects of your branding. But it makes a lot of sense to see what others do and to be inspired by it. You will find a lot of dross amongst the image search results but also one or two designs that are head and shoulders above the others. What is it about them that means they look so much better (hint: nine times out of ten, you'll instantly know the answer to that if you've read "The Non-Designers Design Book").

Using this approach means you spot trends in your industry and by looking at the labelling and other artwork of the premium products, you get an idea of what your customers are looking for.

Case Study 1: MakingYourOwnCandles.co.uk

At MYOC, we use various strategies and tools for each of the graphic elements we use:

Logo: Our original logo was "done on the cheap" for £25 and was bloody awful. We had it replaced with one that was posted as a project on 99designs.co.uk

Stickers, labels, leaflets etc: I create these in Adobe Illustrator (I have a subscription to the Adobe Creative Cloud service due to my other businesses in web design and programming) and output them as PDFs. These are uploaded to Printed.com for digital printing.

Instruction sheets: These are created using Serif PagePlus, saved as PDFs and some are printed on our colour laser printer, those for our most popular products are sent to Printed.com as they work out cheaper for larger quantities.

Case Study 2: Say it with Brownies (SayitwithBrownies.co.uk)

How did you go premium?

> "My pricing was based on what I felt the market would accept.
> There are more expensive and cheaper mail order brownies out
> there, but none have my unique selling point of having the
> customisable gift packaging. Therefore I felt I could command a
> small premium. Also I wanted to set a price that would allow me to
> do promotions with voucher codes as I know that people love a
> 'deal'. It was easy to research the market, I found every competitor I
> could on the internet and made a big table of prices and the
> services they offered, then pitched my pricing where I felt was
> appropriate. One of my major competitors would be online flower
> sellers and I felt my brownies needed to be at a lower price than
> sending a bouquet. Finally I knew the costing of my ingredients,
> packaging and postage so understood the parameters I had to
> work within. It's all about knowing your market and your costs,

after that it's quite simple to make a decision."

How do you source your packaging?

"I employed the services of a small marketing agency on the Isle of Wight called Peekaboo Design and they created my brand designs, the packaging designs and my website. I was keen to have one agency handle everything so that I got a very joined up result, with the website and packaging having the same look and feel. Peekaboo also managed the print and sourced suppliers for me. I now have the pdf files and simply reorder items as I need them."

Do you outsource your design work?

"I outsourced my design work as it isn't my strength, I'm a good project manager and am good at delivering a service, but visual creativity isn't really my thing. For a truly professional result I knew I needed to get some expert help from a designer."

Case Study: Littlecote Soap Co (www.littlecotesoap.co.uk)

How do you source your packaging?

> "Lots and lots of searching on the internet! To start with I used off the shelf companies selling ready-made boxes such as Fold-a-Box, Bag & Box Man, The Tiny Box Company (I first saw them on Dragon's Den), Midpac, Keylink (supplier to the Chocolate industry), Club Green and Italian Options (ribbons, organza bags, favour boxes), 3A Manufacturing (eco-friendly bubble bags). These days I have bespoke boxes made for me and I attend packaging trade shows such as Packaging Innovations where many manufacturers exhibit."

Do you outsource your design work?

> "I have always printed my own labels on a laser printer. However this year we have purchased a digital printer (a Primera from KTEC) which is used by many small manufacturers. I also use Vistaprint - you can design the labels or leaflets yourself, they are quick and cheap to purchase, and they are printed in colour. We have loads of different types of labels which is why we produce most of them ourselves. However, if you have only a few labels of each type it might be worth looking into getting them printed, especially if you want a special finish.
>
> For our bespoke boxes, I employ a freelance designer who has all of the professional equipment to be able to create print-ready artwork for the manufacturer."

In summary, then – yes you can do it yourself but be prepared to spend a lot of time learning!

INVEST IN INGREDIENTS

Okay, so you've created attractive packaging. I can't get much more specific about exactly what will work for your particular craft because it varies so much – the best approach is to find examples within your own industry of premium products and see how they present themselves.

But, at the end of the day, it's the product that's premium – the packaging is just a signal. If, on opening the box, bag or whatever, the product inside is distinctly ordinary, the spell is broken. You can't have sizzle without sausage.

Organics

If appropriate to your craft, you can include organic ingredients to increase the quality and perceived value of the product. Soap making is one example, but this is also true of all food and drink-based craft products. Be careful to make certain that the ingredients really are organic if you're going to pass on the claim. All reputable suppliers will be able to provide specific information on how their ingredients are created and which standards they conform to.

Eco-friendly

Many of the ingredients used across a number of crafts are derived from the oil and other fossil fuel industries. They also happen to be the cheapest, usually, so by using a non-fossil alternative, you increase the value of the product. Eco-Soya wax is one such example.

There are two things to be careful of, however. Firstly, before you make claims, be sure of your facts – the ecological impact of eco-soya, for example, isn't necessarily straightforward[1]. If in doubt, don't add direct claims. Frankly, in this case, the name of the ingredient is enough to make the connection.

Secondly, be aware that by choosing alternative ingredients, you need to thoroughly test that your product performs as well after the switch.

[1]   For example, has the soy crop been sown on land cleared from jungle or forest? Have you taken into account how far it has travelled to get to you? Would paraffin wax produced in the UK actually have a lower environmental impact (given that it's a by-product of the oil industry rather than its reason for existing) than eco-soya brought in by container ship from half way around the world? I don't know the answer to this – I'm just making the point that it's not quite as simple as it might seem at first.

Eco-soya wax, and others that are naturally derived, behave and burn differently to paraffin waxes affecting the appearance and characteristics of the product. Customers who've paid extra for an eco-friendly product, expect to get at least the same performance.

Fair-trade

As with the others, you need to be sure of the credentials of any materials you purchase under the fair-trade banner. If so, then by all means make a song and dance in your promotional literature about the hand-made jute bag containing your creation. Crafters and their customers are a generous and kind lot, overall, and many will be prepared to pay a little extra for a product that benefits someone in the third world.

Rare ingredients

You can add a premium slant, and price, to your product by including exotic ingredients –rare spices in chutneys, unusual fruits in jams, expensive essential oils in perfume scents, candles or soaps. Just be careful – these ingredients can eat heavily into your profit margin. One option is to choose a similar but cheaper ingredient. The classic example of this is to use cedarwood essential oil rather than sandalwood (which costs 25x as much!) for a similar effect at a fraction of the cost.

These are just a few ways you can change a product to make it premium.

Don't forget that, aside from changing the recipe and adding nice packaging, you can also add value to the product by introducing an element of customisation or personalisation so that the customer feels their product is, more or less, unique. Similarly, creating scarcity by offering limited editions of your products encourages people to buy more quickly. Alternatively, by organising your products into collections, some customers will wish to buy the complete set over time.

There are dozens of ways to turn an ordinary product into a premium one. The key is to make sure that you are adding value to it – the end result must be a better product whether it's intrinsically better or more eco-friendly, for example. The job of the packaging is to signal to customers that you have something special for them – that something must be special otherwise they'll be disappointed both in the product and you.

TOTTING IT UP

One final note. Don't forget to include the cost of the packaging in the cost price, along with any adjustments for going premium (although, hopefully, you'll have been targeting the higher end of the market from the beginning). Once you've done this, apply your markup to the true cost price and you'll have your new retail price.

Bear in mind that, although your margin remains the same in percentage terms, the amount of real cash you take goes up. If the true cost price of your product goes up from £2.50 to £4.50 through the changes in packaging and ingredients, your selling price would go from around £4.40 for the original product up to £7.85 for the premium one and your net profit increases from £1.90 per unit to £3.35, an increase of nearly 80%.

You could also experiment with higher margins for your premium products – at the end of the day it's a combination of what you feel comfortable with (although you should never decrease your margin) and what customers will pay.

MILESTONE 4: GET IT PREMIUMED

Your product is now ready to be dressed to thrill so it's time to get the packaging organised and make any necessary adjustments to the ingredients and other aspects of its presentation. Remember to update the cost price if required and, based on that, update the selling price to reflect your product's premium status.

Having said all that – not every product needs to be right at the top end of the market. The work you've done getting packaging sorted for your premium offerings, however, can be put to good use for the rest of the range. Don't dally with the bottom of the market, however – the rest of the range should be firmly in the middle of the price bracket.

You mid-range products will need to have their packaging toned down so that they can be produced more cheaply – otherwise you'll be eating into your profit margin for your cheaper products. It's essential, throughout, that you maintain a clear design distinction between mid-market and top of the range products.

Most of us can only develop one product at a time, or at most a small related range of similar products. I believe that, for the first products you create, you should concentrate on the premium end of the market if at all possible. This is the most profitable place to be and it establishes your products as part of a quality brand. If you then choose to introduce a slightly cheaper range then fine but the danger is that if you begin with mid-range products, your only direction in terms of price might be downwards. A premium brand can easily introduce a "value" mid-market range – it's much harder to go the other way.

You've got it. Flaunt it.

CHAPTER 6: SETTING UP YOUR OFFICE

We've created our products, wrapped them in nice packaging and priced them for maximum profits. It's now time to turn our attention to the nitty gritty of getting up and running from home.

YOUR HOME OFFICE

There's no getting away from the face that you'll need at least a little space dedicated to your business. You need space for three purposes: production, stock/fulfilment and space for running the business.

PRODUCTION SPACE

This is where you'll be making your products – you need somewhere to actually work and somewhere to store partially made creations. The amount of room this needs depends very much on the particular craft you've chosen but it should be dedicated to the purpose. At a push, you can keep your regularly used materials and tools in crate which you can then get out as needed and easily shove out of the way when finished.

The more messy the production process, the greater the need for space out of the house – whether that's a shed, garage or even just a foldable table on the deck.

In our case, we started MakingYourOwnCandles in a house that had a good sized kitchen so we used a corner of that for production in the early days. We quickly outgrew this arrangement and, when we moved to the south coast 6 months later, picked a house with a garage. This has been steadily converted to a workshop with shelving, cupboard space and, most recently, a stud wall blocking in the garage door to both insulate it and give space for an additional workbench. This means that, during busy periods, several people can work in the same space.

At some point, you may well find your business is too large to be based at home and the next logical step is to hire space in one of the increasingly common business parks with flexible leases. These allow you to rent an office or light industrial workshop on a monthly basis with all costs (rates, broadband, heating etc) included in a single fee.

We're likely to face the choice, in 2013, of whether to go this way or move again – the price of success!

SPACE FOR STOCK & FULFILMENT

Don't overlook the need to have somewhere dry and, often, cool to store the products you've made – whether that's to stock your internet shop or in preparation for a farmer's market or craft fair.

If you sell online, you also need somewhere to prepare your orders for despatch and to keep them before taking them to the post office or while awaiting collection. A kitchen table can be pressed into service for this but ideally, it'll be near to where your stock is kept.

SPACE TO RUN THE BUSINESS

Red tape and record keeping are a fact of all businesses and you need somewhere to both carry out this work and to keep your records organised. We bought an old filing cabinet from our local Barnado's shop and Peta's enjoyed hyper-organising the filing pockets (which is just as well as I'd be hopeless at it!).

It's absolutely essential to keep your paperwork somewhere safe, secure and dry because you can be sure it'll be the supplier invoice you've lost that you'll need at some point.

If you're not lucky enough to have a spare room available, a kitchen table will serve as an office desk. In this case, it's again a good idea to keep your office tools in a crate so it can be stowed away when not in use.

GETTING EQUIPPED

LAPTOP

A laptop is likely to be the best choice for most businesses when they first set up (don't be tempted to use a tablet, such as an iPad, Nexus 7 or Kindle Fire, instead of a laptop, you'll end up very frustrated). [1]

The good news is that decent laptops have never been cheaper and, whilst there's a massive range to choose from, it's actually very easy to narrow down the choices.

[1] Having said that, if you have a dedicated space available, you'll get more "bang for your buck" with a desktop computer than a laptop.

Budget

How much do you need to spend? Around £350 will get you a capable laptop that will serve your business for several years.

Manufacturer

I recommend you only buy from a manufacturer you've heard of. Good choices include Samsung, HP, Toshiba, Acer, Asus, Sony and Dell.

You'll probably notice that I haven't included Apple in this list. This is because, for all their other qualities, they do not represent the best value for money on the market – the cheapest MacBook with a screen large enough to be usable as a business computer (the MacBook Air 13 inch) starts at around £1,000. If you happen to have an Apple computer, on the other hand, that's fine.

Specification

The three main things to look out for are the monitor size, RAM and processor. Most laptops have a widescreen ratio, similar to a TV, since they're designed for playing movies as well as for work. For most purposes, the ideal screen size is 15.6-inch – this is big enough to be usable, whilst not being too large to easily lug around.

RAM is the short term memory of a laptop – if you buy one with too little memory, it will slow down when you're running several programmes at once. RAM is measured in gigabytes (GB) and all you need to remember is to make sure you get a laptop with at least 4GB.

The most important part of the specification to insist on is the processor. There is a bewildering range available, all in various versions but it all boils down to the following: if your budget is £350 or so, make sure you get an Intel Core i3. If your budget is £500, get an Intel Core i5. Exactly which variety you get doesn't matter – just go for those models and you are making a safe choice.

The laptop will come with a version of Windows – as long as it's either Windows 7 or Windows 8 that's fine. Do not pay extra for a Windows 8 laptop assuming Windows 8 is better – for our purposes it is not. However, do make sure you get the "64 bit" version – don't worry about what this is exactly, just look for it in the laptop description.

Where to buy it
Personally, I almost always buy technology from Amazon. It's usually the cheapest and, in my experience, handles returns very well indeed.

You will find a small selection of suitable laptops in the £350-£500 price range at **www.yourcraftbusiness.co.uk**

I can't afford £350!
If your budget won't stretch to £350 and you need to buy a laptop then the second hand market is a good alternative. I don't recommend buying from individuals, either directly or via eBay as you could end up having been sold a dud.

A better idea is to get a professionally refurbished laptop from a reputable supplier. I recommend Morgan Computers (**www.morgancomputers.co.uk**) or Laptops Direct (**www.laptopsdirect.co.uk**), both of whom I've used personally. Bear in mind that you'll also need to lower your specification requirements to find a laptop significantly cheaper than £350. Depending on stock, it should be possible to find a serviceable model at around the £250 mark, but when you get below £200 the laptop is likely to be old and slow as, at that price, they're usually ex-corporate machines.

At an absolute bare minimum, aim for an Intel Core 2 Duo processor – do not get anything labelled "Pentium", "Celeron" or "Intel Dual Core".

If you're really strapped for cash, then a desktop computer will offer better value. A usable Dell Optiplex Mini Tower costs £125 at the time of writing (at Morgan Computers), although you'd need to add £50 or so for a refurbished monitor.

PRINTER
You'll need a printer of some sort both for correspondence and producing packing slips and invoices. You may well also want to use it for packaging.

If you only ever intend to use it for office work, then just about any inkjet printer will suffice. Avoid those that have a single colour cartridge – by choosing one with separate tanks you can replace each colour as it runs out rather than chucking the whole cartridge when the first colour expires.

We tend to buy Canon inkjets – they tend to be amongst the best performing and offer good value – but it makes sense to buy an all-in-one printer, scanner and photocopier and the best value at present is the HP Photosmart 5510 (there's a link at **www.yourcraftbusiness.co.uk**).

If you *do* intend to print packaging and leaflets using your printer then I recommend a colour laser – for three reasons. Firstly, running costs are lower, especially for pages that use a lot of colour. Secondly, the quality of the end results is higher – close to those you'd get by using a professional printing firm. Finally, as I mentioned earlier, laser toner is waterproof whereas inkjet ink runs at the slightest provocation.

I recommend the Lexmark C540n which, as well as being at the lower end of the price spectrum, is not only networkable so you can connect to it from multiple computers and around the house, but is a single-pass printer which makes it ideal for specialist paper printing.

If you are only going to be printing fairly standard papers then Samsung's CLP-325 is a good alternative.

NETWORKING

Until fairly recently there were just two options for at-home networking – you either went entirely wireless or ran network cable around the house.

The problem with wireless networking is that you might well be unable to get a decent signal from every location in the house. It's also (in the real world) slower than cabled networking and less stable.

Fortunately, there's a simple answer – PowerLine networking. This works by sending network traffic through your mains power circuit. All you do is buy a minimum of two network adaptors and plug one into the mains socket nearest your broadband router, linking them together using the network cable provided with the adaptor. Now, plug another adaptor into the mains near your computer and connect them together using another network cable. What happens is that the computer sends network traffic down its cable, into the adaptor. It then gets sent around the mains until it finds the other adaptor and it then travels up the cable from that one and into the router.

It really is very simple – and needs, in most cases, no configuration at all. Your computer will immediately pick up the new network and start using it. If you work in two places, simply buy another network adaptor and plug it in- again, it'll work automatically.

When it comes to choosing one, just make sure it has a minimum quoted speed of 200 MBPS. There's a link to a suitable starter kit at www.yourcraftbusiness.co.uk.

WORKING IN THE CLOUD

The "cloud" is a term used to describe hard disk space that's amalgamated and made available over the internet. Until very recently, a home based business would use Network Attached Storage (basically a large hard disk accessible to all computers) as its primary way of sharing files between computers. Indeed, this is still a good choice if your broadband connection is slow.

The problem with NAS is that it's a physical device that can break (or be stolen). By using "cloud" services, you get away from having your data on a single device as it's shared and mirrored across the industrial servers of providers such as Google and Microsoft.

The biggest day to day advantage, however, is that by using the cloud, you can work on any device you like, from any location you like.

Let's take an example. Dropbox is a very popular cloud service and includes a free option. Once installed, it sets up a special folder on your computer called, not surprisingly, "Dropbox" and everything that you put in that folder gets copied, in the background, to their server. So, if you create a folder inside the dropbox folder containing, for example, your business correspondence or packaging designs, they exist not only on your laptop but also on dropbox's server. Every time you make a change, the new file is copied up there without you even knowing it.

Now imagine your laptop broke. Without Dropbox (or some other backup strategy) you'd have lost everything. But since you used Dropbox, all you have to do is install it on another computer, log in and it will automatically copy down your files onto the new computer. Furthermore, Dropbox apps exist for just about all smartphones and tablets so you can view and edit documents from your iPad should the mood take you.

Google and Microsoft each have their own systems. If you're going to be creating a lot of documents Google Drive is worth looking at. It works in broadly the same way as Dropbox except that it's integrated into Google Docs (their free equivalent of Microsoft Office). So, as you're creating and editing documents using Google Docs, they're being automatically created and updated on Google Drive. This means, in practice, that you can view and edit your documents from any internet enabled device – usually without needing to install anything at all since Google Docs works within a browser window.

We use Google Drive and Google Docs as our primary office and organisational software for MakingYourOwnCandles. All word processed documents and spreadsheets are created using the Google Docs tools and we use Google Drive as our central repository of files, including all artwork, photos and instructions leaflets.

BACKING UP TO THE CLOUD
When you start your own business, you need to take the safety of your data very seriously. It's not good enough to have it on just one computer. By itself, using Dropbox or Google Drive solves part of the backup problem – it means that if your own hardware fails, you can easily retrieve your business data by simply installing Dropbox, for example, on another computer and logging in.

However, backup has another role – protecting you from accidental deletion. If you deleted a file in your Dropbox folder, it will also be deleted from their servers. So you need a second line of defence so that you have a proper backup.

There are two options. If you're using Google Drive then it's easy – sign up for the Backupify service (www.backupify.com) and they will back up the entire contents of your Google Drive, including Google Docs documents, to a new location on a regular basis, enabling you to retrieve the previous version of any file. This really is very simple and it's the best solution I've come across for hassle free backup.

Dropbox adopts a slightly different approach in that it keeps all the versions of your files for 30 days so, as long as you visit the Dropbox website within that time, you can rescue any accidentally deleted files.

Whatever you do, you must have a backup strategy – the authorities can ask for documents going back several years.

OFFICE SOFTWARE

Lots of people have copies of Microsoft Office lying around but be sure to only use properly licensed software with your business.

If you have a Google account (for example, for gmail) you'll have access to Google Docs which provides all the functionality most small businesses need. To get this sign up for Google Apps (http://www.google.com/enterprise/apps/business/pricing.html) and select the Free option – this has absolutely everything you're likely ever to need.

If you're going to be doing a lot of writing or spreadsheet work, you might prefer more fully featured software and in that case I recommend LibreOffice (www.libreoffice.org) is a free, Microsoft compatible, office suite that will easily handle anything you're likely to throw at it. You might have heard of OpenOffice – LibreOffice is the free, open source version of that long-established suite.

Remember that if you save into a Dropbox or Google Drive folder, your documents are backed up to the cloud and can be accessed from any PC with the correct login credentials. For most craft business, a simple Dropbox or Google Drive setup will suffice for sharing and backing up without the need for any extra technology.

BEING CONTACTABLE

The two main ways of being contactable are by phone and email. Fortunately, technology makes both of these simple and very cheap.

Phone

When I started my first business back in 1999, the only option was to have several phone lines installed at great expense. Today, things are very different. You can, of course, use a mobile phone to handle all your business calls – but this means either having a second handset for business or giving out your personal number. I don't know about you, but however much I may like my customers, I don't want them ringing me in the middle of the night to ask why they can't get their candle out of the mould!

The simple answer to your telecommunication problems is Skype. Now, I don't mean that you should expect your customers to have to use their computers or mobile devices to call your Skype name – there is a much better way. Skype allows you have your own phone number (you select from a range of available numbers) so that customers can use their standard phone to ring you. You set up the system so that it directs all calls to your mobile phone. The customer has no idea they're ringing a mobile and your mobile number remains private. It's not free (it costs around £3 per month) but it's far, far cheaper than having a landline put in and you can cancel at any time. This is the approach I now use for all my businesses.

Find out more at **http://www.skype.com/intl/en-gb/features/allfeatures/online-number/** or, as always, at **www.yourcraftbusiness.co.uk**

Email

There are plenty of places to get a free email account (the best, in my view, is still gmail) but it's essential that you can send and receive email from your website address. For now, remember that it's simple enough for you (or your web designer) to set things up so that you can use your gmail account to send and receive emails from your website address.

Case Study: MakingYourOwnCandles (www.makingyourowncandles.co.uk)

For general office work we use Google Docs – mainly the word processor and spreadsheet. Whilst Google Docs is available to all gmail users, if you want to be able to share documents within your business, you'll need to sign up for Google Apps. There's a free edition but we signed up to Google Apps for Business so that we could use one of our own domain names and various other minor advantages (it costs $5 per user per month). You can find details of both at:

http://www.google.com/enterprise/apps/business/pricing.html

We use Adobe's Creative Cloud products (especially Fireworks and Illustrator) for our artwork needs, and Serif's PagePlus for desktop publishing our instruction leaflets. Serif's DrawPlus and PhotoPlus would have served to replace the Adobe products if we didn't use Creative Cloud for other businesses.

We have a Dymo label printer which we use for adding barcodes and warning labels, and two Lexmark C540 single pass laser printers for inhouse artwork. We also have shrink-wrapping facilities for our Amazon stock.

CHAPTER 7: SETTING UP YOUR BUSINESS

It's time to get "official" - but don't panic as it isn't nearly as complicated as you might imagine. However, for the sake of my legal advisors, please read this disclaimer[1].

---

[1]   I have made every effort to research this area and to translate the advice given on various government websites into the sort of English that humans use. To the best of my knowledge, what I say here is entirely accurate but it's your responsibility to satisfy yourself of the appropriate action to take for your own business. My official advice is to ask an accountant or member of a similar profession before taking any decisions.

AM I A BUSINESS?

This was one of the most often asked questions in the survey that gave rise to this book. If you want to read what HMRC have to say on the matter you can find it here:
http://www.hmrc.gov.uk/manuals/svmanualnew/svm111110.htm and at **www.yourcraftbusiness.co.uk**.

My interpretation of this legalistic guff is that if your craft activity satisfies some or all of the following criteria, you're likely to be considered to be running a "business". For each, I show the HMRC wording followed by my interpretation.

According to HMRC a business:

1. *is "a serious undertaking earnestly pursued" or "a serious occupation, not necessarily confined to commercial or profit-making undertakings"*

    Is it a "serious undertaking"? This probably means, are you giving it serious attention? I suggest that if you carry out the exercises in this book, the answer to this question is probably "yes"

2. *is "an occupation or function actively pursued with reasonable or recognisable continuity"*

    Are you/have you been working on your activity over a reasonable period of continuous time? Of course, this on its own does not make your craft a business.

3. *has "a certain measure of substance as measured by the quarterly or annual value of . . . supplies made"*

    Have you sold any? How much? "a certain measure of substance" represents an unwelcome slice of subjectivity.

4. *was "conducted in a regular manner and on sound and recognised business principles"*

    If it looks like a business and acts like a business, it's probably a business in the eyes of the authorities

5. *is "predominantly concerned with the making of ... supplies to consumers for a consideration"*

    Are your activities designed to sell things to people?

6. *and whether those supplies "are of a kind which, subject to differences in detail, are commonly made by those who seek to profit by them"*

    Have other people run businesses similar to what you're doing?

Seriously, could it be any more opaque? Perhaps an example would help.

Jo Jones is in her kitchen making Strawberry and Blueberry Jam on a wet Sunday afternoon in October. She ends up with 10 jars of lovely home made jam and realises that she's made too much for her own use.

She pops next door and sells a jar to Edna for £2, and subsequently sells another four jars to other neighbours.

Now, I suggest that of the 6 criteria, only the final one would apply to Jo at this stage since there are plenty of jam making businesses around. Otherwise, if I were her, I'd pocket my £10 and relax about whether I'm a business or not.[1]

Let's wind the clock forward a few weeks.

Inspired by the praise she's received for her jam, not to mention the cash potential, Jo has decided to start a part time business making and selling preserves. She decides to begin by renting a table at her local school fete and spends the next few weeks making up dozens of jars-worth of stock.

[1] Sigh. I am required to point out that all extra income should be reported on your tax return.

This involves purchasing glassware and labels from a supplier and having her kitchen inspected and certified by the local Environmental Health officer.

Looking at the 6 criteria, she probably meets 1,4,5 and 6 before the fete takes place, and adds number 3 once she has made some money. I suggest that she is now a business.

But what if the craft fair is a disaster? What if she makes no money at all and decides it's the worst idea she's ever had? Well, firstly you can unregister as a business if necessary. Secondly, I'm not sure she'd need to necessarily register before the fair. If she made no money, HMRC are unlikely to be interested. If she did make a profit then she has a business and should register. This is how I interpret the regulations but she should, at that point, have a chat with an accountant to be certain of the best approach.

AM I SELF-EMPLOYED?

This is a related question, but it's not quite the same thing. Fortunately, it's much more straightforward to answer. These are the tests HMRC uses (**http://www.hmrc.gov.uk/employment-status/index.htm**)

Are you self employed? The answer is (probably) "yes" if the following apply:

- Can they hire someone to do the work or engage helpers at their own expense?

- Do they risk their own money?

- Do they provide the main items of equipment they need to do their job, not just the small tools that many employees provide for themselves?

- Do they agree to do a job for a fixed price regardless of how long the job may take?

- Can they decide what work to do, how and when to do the work and where to provide the services?

- Do they regularly work for a number of different people?

- Do they have to correct unsatisfactory work in their own time and at their own expense?

I suggest that, if you're creating a craft business as outlined in this book, you're likely to meet just about all of those criteria. Bear in mind that, as well as satisfying big brother, by registering as a company you benefit from being able to reduce your tax bill by claiming expenses against the business and other tax-deductable items.

WHAT ABOUT MY EXISTING JOB?
It is perfectly possible to be **both** employed in a regular job **and** self-employed in your own business.

TYPES OF COMPANY
There are, for most purposes, only two types of company – those that are effectively you with a different hat on, and those that are independent entities of their own. The most common route is to start as a sole trader and, in many cases, "upgrade" to limited company status later.

SOLE TRADERS
Most new craft business start as sole traders, and many stay that way permanently. As a sole trader **the business is YOU**. Broadly speaking, what you do is let the tax authorities know you're generating an income through business activities. This allows you to pay a special, lower, national insurance rate and to deduct certain "allowable expenses" from your taxable income

The **advantages** of registering as a sole trader include:

- it's easier to set up and run than any other form of company

- the book-keeping and accountancy regulations are simpler

- you get to keep all the profits

- your data is kept private (limited companies are on a publicly available register)

However, there are some **disadvantages**

- the company's debts are your debts – there is no separation between what the company owes and what you owe

- as you're the only one who can control the business, if you're unavailable (through illness, for example) the company grinds to a halt unless you have some form of covenant in place

- other businesses and, to a degree, the public see sole traders as less secure or credible as businesses. This depends largely on the sort of craft business you set up.

Partnerships
These are a special form of company that's essentially the same as the sole trader but for multiple owners. To form a partnership, you need to have a partnership agreement drawn up so they're not as simple as sole trading.

The big problem with partnerships is that in the event of something going wrong, you are liable not only for your own share of the debts of the business, but also those of your partners. History is full of stories of mugs who got left with massive debts when partners scarpered leaving them to face the music.

My strong advice is not to consider a partnership – they're a disaster waiting to happen.

LIMITED COMPANIES
Limited companies are, in the eyes of the law, "separate legal entities". They're set up with shareholders who own the company and directors who run it – in your case it's likely that there will be one shareholder

(you) owning one share and one director (you). But the money in the company bank account is not technically yours, although you control it.

A limited company is taxed separately and you, as director, draw a salary and extract profits through dividends.

The main **advantages** of a limited company are:

- You and the business are separate – the business's debts are **not** your debts. However, this isn't quite the advantage you might imagine because most lenders will expect you to personally guarantee any borrowing.

- You will **usually** pay less personal tax if you run a limited company. Most directors pay themselves a salary of roughly the same amount as the personal allowance (just over £8,000 in 2012) which means they pay no tax or national insurance on that amount and additional income is paid in the form of dividends which are, effectively, free of any personal tax. On the other hand, the company itself pays tax on its profits but because this is currently around 20% in total, the amount paid overall is lower.[1]

- Limited companies are seen by many to have more credibility

The **disadvantages** include:

- They're slightly more involved to set up (but, honestly, not much)

- Companies must file certain paperwork every year and get fined heavily if they miss deadlines. Because of the rigid and complex format of company accounts, this means you really **must** hire an accountant if you form a limited company. Frankly, you **should** hire an accountant whatever form of company you choose but, for some reason, accountants tend to charge much lower rates for sole traders.

[1]   In general – ask your accountant about your own situation!

- Closing a limited company down is significantly more involved than shutting up shop as a sole trader

TaxCafe (**www.taxcafe.co.uk**) has an excellent range of books – including some covering tax for the self-employed and those for company directors. Whilst I strongly recommend having an accountant handle your taxation, it is a very good idea to know what the taxation issues are, at least in general.

WHAT SHOULD I CALL MY COMPANY?

Broadly speaking, pretty much anything you like. The rules are a little stricter for Limited Companies than Sole Traders but the main requirement is that you don't seek to pass yourself off as another company (or, indeed, the government). You also can't use offensive words (surprise).

Bearing in mind that you might want to become a limited company later, even if you start as a sole trader, it makes sense to choose a name that will work for both. Begin by going to the WebCheck service at Companies House (**http://www.companieshouse.gov.uk/info**) and type your chosen company name into the search box. The system will list all similar names so you can make sure your preferred option isn't taken.

You should also go to the Intellectual Property Office and search amongst registered trade marks to see if, by sheer bad luck, someone's registered a trade mark similar to your company name. If they have, and you create a company with that name, you could be forced to change it later, which is an administrative nightmare as well as causing untold damage to your website, reputation and marketing literature.

Go to **http://www.ipo.gov.uk/tm/t-find/t-find-text/** to conduct the search. The chances are, nothing will come up, but it's worth checking right at the beginning.

REGISTERING AS A SOLE TRADER

Once you've decided to start up in business as a sole trader, the process is pretty straightforward.

Begin by going to
https://online.hmrc.gov.uk/registration/newbusiness/introduction
. Bear in mind that, as part of this process, you must register for the
Government Gateway (by clicking the **Create an account for me** link
at the bottom of the page) and this involves them sending you an
activation code through the post so it takes a few days.

Follow the process through and you'll be self employed!

In practice what this means is that you will be sent a self-assessment
form to complete each tax year. If you are also still in employment then
you'll simply use the information on your year end P60 to fill the details
of that employment in, along with information about your self
employment. It's not rocket science, but I recommend having an
accountant do it – he or she is likely to save you more money than they
charge in fees.

HMRC provides guidance and links on the procedure at
http://www.hmrc.gov.uk/selfemployed/register-selfemp.htm

There's information on how you go about closing a business (from the
HMRC point of view) at
http://www.hmrc.gov.uk/dealingwith/changes/close-sell-business.htm
– in case you want to reassure yourself that this isn't too difficult if it
doesn't work out.

REGISTERING AS A LIMITED COMPANY

I recommend doing this either through your new accountant (don't go
limited without one) or one of the many online services that carry out
the work. We used company-wizard.co.uk to form
MakingYourOwnCandles.co.uk.

DOING THE BOOKS

This is not a book about book-keeping but I'd like you to have an idea of what you're responsible for, as a business owner. I'm going to assume you're a sole trader for now (since most of the readers of this book will start that way) but almost everything I have to say applies whatever form of business you choose.

BOOK-KEEPING SOFTWARE

The first thing you should do, once you've registered yourself as self employed, is to sign up for an online book-keeping service. This isn't a service that does your book-keeping for you (although you could opt for that – there are good reasons for not doing so[1]) but a web application that helps you do it for yourself and safely stores your information online.

I strongly recommend that you choose a tool called FreeAgent (there's a link at www.yourcraftbusiness.co.uk which includes a 10% discount). I use FreeAgent for all four of my limited companies and it has revolutionised the way I do my book-keeping. I'm not exaggerating. When I set up my first company, I employed someone part time to do the book-keeping using the industry standard of the time: Sage.

As I set up other companies, I learned to use Sage. I also learned to hate it. A VAT return would take at least a full working day to sort out. So I tried FreeAgent – I now do my book-keeping only when a VAT return is due and it takes around 90 minutes (every three months) to update my book-keeping per company.

FreeAgent works by allowing you to upload your electronic bank statements (all banks allow you to export them in a format that FreeAgent can read) and then asking you to indicate what category each entry goes under – no need for the dreaded double-entry book-keeping! As time goes on, FreeAgent learns about your regular transactions so you end up having to manually mark up fewer and fewer, and the process becomes quicker each time.

When it's time to have your tax return completed, you can either give

---

[1] I believe a business owner should, if at all possible, do their own book-keeping. Modern online services make this very fast and simple – by doing it yourself you get an intimate view of how your business is doing that is hard to achieve just by looking at reports.

your accountant limited access to FreeAgent or, as in my case, export your book-keeping into a format they can easily use to prepare your return.

There are other services that appear to offer similar functionality, but if you want a personal recommendation formed over several years of using the service, then go for FreeAgent (click the link at www.yourcraftbusiness.co.uk).

And, as a final note, if your accountant tries to convince you to use Sage (after all he/she probably has years invested in it) then find another accountant. Sage has created this great myth that book-keeping is difficult, and this suits some accountants – remember you are the client and you'd be better off spending your time building your business rather than chained to a desk battling with Sage.

WHAT RECORDS TO KEEP

HMRC provides a list of the sorts of records you must keep at http://www.hmrc.gov.uk/sa/rec-keep-self-emp.htm (links at www.yourcraftbusiness.co.uk).

Broadly speaking these include

- cashbooks

- invoices

- mileage records

- bank statements (only if you don't have online banking)

- receipts for purchases you make

- P60s if you're also employed

- any other evidence of income or expense related to the business.

You must keep these records for six years at least.

One benefit of buying as much as you possibly can online is that you will receive an invoice by email. If you use an online email service such as gmail, this forms a backup of that receipt, which means you'll only lose it if you delete it.

From this basic data, FreeAgent will create your business books and, from them, everything that's needed to file your return.

TAX AND RUNNING A BUSINESS

Whilst you will need to consult your accountant about the detail, it's useful to know what you can generally claim.

National Insurance and Income Tax

The rules for income generated from self-employment are slightly different to those from a regular job. As you and the business are one and the same, you get the same personal allowance as everyone else – which means (in the 2012/13 tax year) that the first £8,105 of your income is free of income tax. If your income is less than £7,605 then you also pay no Class 4 National Insurance and if it's less than £5,595 you pay no Class 2 National Insurance (which is only £2.65 per week anyway).

It gets a whole lot more complicated if you are starting up your business alongside a paid job. However, that's what accountants (and accountancy software) are for! My advice – leave it to the experts.

Use of home

Most home businesses, even very small ones, can claim back a proportion of their household expenses. Again, your accountant is the best person to help you with this but this can make a significant difference to the amount of tax you pay. You can claim a proportion of your household expenses based on the amount of floor space your business occupies or what percentage of the rooms in the house it occupies.

What household expenses? Most of them – including mortgage interest (or rent), utility bills, council tax, insurance and even the cost of maintaining and cleaning the house. You can also claim back the cost of your telephone and broadband although in that case you'd probably be better off working out a higher proportion as the likelihood is that your business activities will greatly increase their use.

The amount you can claim for a business is proportional to the time spent working in it – a business you work 10 hours a week on will be able to claim less than a full time business.

So, make sure you discuss this with your accountant at your first meeting – many business owners under-use this aspect of taxation, even though it's completely legitimate.

One final thing. Make sure that no room in your house ever becomes purely and solely for the use of the business. If it does, that room will become liable for business rates (and they tend to be higher than council tax) and it can complicate selling your house. To avoid this being an issue, you just need to have something in the room that is clearly of a domestic nature – whether this is a sofa bed or washing machine. Check with your accountant.

There's a good article on this on the FreeAgent site: **http://www.freeagent.com/central/home-as-office?searched=home**

(also at **www.yourcraftbusiness.co.uk**)

Where to find an accountant
As with so many aspects of life, a personal recommendation is best – if you're certain that the person making the recommendation is truly happy with the service they're receiving. Lots of people will recommend whoever they use, partly because they want to be able to help and partly to validate their own choice.

If you're going to use FreeAgent (you are, aren't you?), you could look at their list of accountants at **http://www.freeagent.com/partners** .

In my view, you should be looking for a fixed price service. These range in price from around £20 per month for a simple business up to £50 per month. Services at this price level will take your electronic book-keeping and prepare your tax return or company return (for limited companies). You should be able to have a meeting up front, free of charge, to get some advice. You should use this meeting to ask every question you've got (write them down beforehand and make notes during the meeting), to make sure you understand exactly what the service offers and to work out whether you feel you can get on with the accountant and their firm.

There are good accountants and poor accountants, as with all professions – which is why it's so essential to meet them in person. You'll soon catch a whiff of the barnyard if they're not up to snuff. If they can't very ably explain which expenses you can claim for working at home then scratch them off the list.

CHAPTER 8: OPENING UP FOR BUSINESS

REGULATION, REGULATION, REGULATION

Depending on the nature of your craft business, you may need to comply with government regulations – in the main intended to protect the public. This needs to be done ahead of your starting to trade as a business.

FOOD BUSINESSES

Quite why it's so hard to find clear, detailed guidance for this I don't know. The best summary I can find is at **http://scrib.me/ycbfood** – whilst this is an archive page it is still linked to from the Food Standard Agency website (**www.food.gov.uk**)

If you're starting up a business making jam and other preserves, you will need to contact your local authority and have them inspect your food preparation area. This needn't be onerous and you don't need to have a formal qualification in Food Hygiene – you just need to be able to demonstrate that you understand it and have the facilities to carry it out.

Before booking your inspection, download and read the hygiene guide for business here: **http://scrib.me/ycbhygiene** (as always, the link is also on the **www.yourcraftbusiness.co.uk** website).

Here's the crucial passage:

"One of the key requirements of the law is that you must be able to show what you do to make or sell food that is safe to eat and have this written down."

So, you must not only be able to **show** the inspector that you make food safely, you must also have the process **written down** for both your own use and that of any staff.

The process shouldn't be too difficult – Anita from **www.sayitwithbrownies.co.uk** says: "Before I could begin I had to get a food hygiene check from my local council. As we'd just had a new kitchen fitted when we moved house this was all very straight forward and I was given the full five star rating."

Just make sure you get approved *before* you make your first batch of food products for sale to consumers.

Labelling

There are specific guidelines for labelling food products. You can find a guidelines document at **http://scrib.me/ychlabels** (or at **www.yourcraftbusiness.co.uk**) – the practical help begins on page 8.

SOAP AND COSMETICS

Given the range of ingredients used in soap making and the damage they could do in the wrong hands, it's hardly surprising that you need to comply with various regulations if you intend to sell to the public.

The document linked to from the Department for Business, Innovation and Skills covers the most recent regulations which were enacted in 2008. There's a copy here: http://scrib.me/ycbsoap or at www.yourcraftbusiness.co.uk but the best place to start is the website of the Cosmetic, Toiletry & Perfumery Association (www.ctpa.org.uk). Specifically, take a look at the "How are cosmetics regulated?" section at http://www.ctpa.org.uk/content.aspx?pageid=293

The bottom line is that you must have all your products tested by a qualified assessor and include certain statutory information with each. The regulations are changing with effect July 2013 so it's important to keep up to date with them via the CTPA.

Case Study: Littlecote Soap Co (www.littlecoatsoap.co.uk)

What regulations do you have to be aware of?

"I am in the toiletries industry, which comes under the pharmaceutical EU Regulations. Even the smallest company has to have a "Safety Assessment" a cosmetic chemist/toxicologist and have to adhere to very strict labelling, record keeping, weights and measures (we have to have trading standards approved scales).

Even if you are selling very small amounts of a product, you must make sure that you are adhering to the regulations for your industry. If in doubt, contact your local trading standards office who will advise you. Make sure that your product is labelled correctly and if the law requires it, include weights and measures, best before dates, manufacturers' details, health and safety information/warnings, directions for use etc.

I have seen products at craft shows that are in breach of copyright laws, so be careful not to produce products that copy existing brands such as bracelets that look like high street brand sweets, or products with Disney characters, etc. as Trading Standards could visit your show. Make sure that if your product looks like food, and is not, that you put "do not eat" on your product. When displaying your products on your stand make sure that children cannot access any product that is dangerous."

OTHER CRAFTS

Many craft products will need to include information (often as a label) to describe how the product should be used safely. For example, if you sell candles, you'll need to attached a candle safety label to each. The format of these stickers varies from craft to craft and the best approach is to check with any trade or regulatory body. At the end of the day, it's your responsibility to give your customers the information they might reasonably need to use your product effectively and safely.

'ELF AND SAFETY

Don't get caught out – read the Health and Safety Executive's leaflet (http://www.hse.gov.uk/pubns/indg449.pdf). You will find that many of the regulations apply only to companies bigger than yours (at the beginning, in any case) but you should read it through to make sure you comply.

INSURING YOUR BUSINESS

At the barest minimum, you will almost certainly need Public Liability and Products Liability insurance (some policies are simply called Public Liability but cover both). This will cover you for claims made by members of the public in, for example, visiting where you work as well as claims made as a result of using your products.

You should seriously consider a specific Home Business policy which includes Public and Products Liability as well as cover for contents, theft and if you're forced to stop trading due to an "insured event" (a flood for example). In our experience these insurance products are not expensive.

The best approach is to talk to an insurance broker specialising in this sort of work. Aviva has a list of brokers here: http://www.aviva.co.uk/yourbusiness/whats-your-business/. Alternatively, if you don't feel you need a broker, you could consider Direct Line's Home Business policy at http://www.directlineforbusiness.co.uk/home-business-insurance

All these links are also at www.yourcraftbusiness.co.uk so you can access them from your computer. Oh, and by the way, if you employ anyone (other than directors of the business) you must, by law, have Employer's Liability Insurance.

FINDING SUPPLIERS

Fortunately, the internet makes it simple to research suppliers. One very good clue of a company's standing in their industry is their ranking on a Google search. This is because this ranking is strongly influenced by how many other **reputable** sites link to them. If you know someone else in your line of work, then ask them – a personal recommendation is about as good as it gets (if it's an honest one).

FIRST IMPRESSIONS COUNT

Whilst you shouldn't write off a potential supplier on your first visit based on the quality of their site – it can tell you a lot about them. If the site looks unloved and rarely updated then be very wary – you want suppliers who are able to reliably provide their products and for whom it is a serious business. What this means in practice is that it's often better to stick to a small number of larger suppliers for the critical materials you need.

START SMALL

Once you find one or more suppliers, place a small order with each so you can assess the order process, how fast and reliably deliveries arrive and how helpful and timely their support is. In fact, it's worth deliberately contacting them using the details on their website, perhaps asking a question about your order, to see how quickly they respond. You may end up working together for a long time, after all.

You will probably find you'll go through many suppliers over time until you settle on a small group of reliable companies. The main frustrations for us have been where the company has been hard to contact, hasn't delivered what they promised when they promised it or where they don't always stock the items we need. Once you get busy, you don't want to have to shop around and find another supplier, so try to settle on your preferred list as soon as possible.

Although your ultimate aim is to buy in big enough quantities to get a bulk discount, err on the side of smaller orders until you're confident in your supplier.

BE NICE

The supplier/customer relationship is very important – it pays to be as polite with your suppliers are you are with your customers, you never know when you're going to need them to help bail you out after you, for example, forget to place that order!

BUT DON'T BE COMPLACENT

Having said that, take the opportunity (during the quiet season in your craft) to look around for alternatives – new companies come into the market all the time, often introducing new technologies or products that could save you money.

GETTING DELIVERED

If you supply your products by post, you'll need to think about the most cost-effective method to use. There's more to this than simply choosing the cheapest – if the delivery method you use has a poor track record, the cost of replacing lost goods and the loss of customer good will is likely to be more expensive by far than any cost savings.

ROYAL MAIL

Maybe we've been lucky, but we have noticed an improvement over the past year in the service we receive from Royal Mail – to the extent that they lose/mangle fewer parcels than any of the other services we've used.

On the other hand, the recent price rises have made them relatively expensive for parcels above a certain weight and you don't get tracking.

If you intend to use Royal Mail, especially if you'll be using the "packet" side for most of your post, then you should consider signing up for a franking machine as soon as possible. This is because franked mail is considerably cheaper than stamped mail. You save over £1 on a 1.01kg parcel sent first class (franked=£4.57, stamps=£5.60 in 2012) so once you start selling a few dozen items a month, the savings can be considerable.

For more information on how to sign up for a franking machine, go to the Royal Mail's site: http://www.royalmail.com/discounts-payment/franking. Bear in mind, however, that Royal Mail is very keen for you to sign up so it's hardly an unbiased point of view.

The way it generally works is that you find a franking machine distributor and sign up through them. We used www.fpmailing.co.uk and chose their entry level machine – the mymail.

FRANKING GOTCHAS

A few things to bear in mind with franking machines:

- They're supplied on a contract, usually 12 months but make sure you know what you're signing up for. We pay around £20 per month.

- You buy credit for the machine in advance. In most cases, the franking machine connects to the supplier via dial-up modem (yes, really) so it needs to be able to reach a phone socket. Believe it or not, these suppliers charge you for the privilege of filling up your machine but include a fixed number of free recharges per year. This is to encourage you to fill up with larger amounts and less regularly – make sure you keep track of how many you've used of your free allowance.

- Franking machines use inkjet-style cartridges (at least, ours does). These cartridges are outrageously expensive to replace – ours costs over £100 for a genuine replacement. However, you can find much cheaper replacements on eBay and online – usually these are refurbished cartridges. Either way, cartridges should print around 4,000 labels each so, assuming you're able to get a refurb for, say, £50, that's just over a penny per label.

- You must post by the date shown on the label (usually the next working day)

- You can add your own logo and message to franked labels, giving a more professional appearance.

So, is it worth it? Let's take a look at an example.

Alison has set up a business providing rug-making supplies. Most of her packages are light – falling into the 0-750g packet range. She sells, on average, 100 products per month.

Paying by stamps, the cost for this is £270 (100 x £2.70).

The cost for franking is more complex to work out but lets assume she is within her free allowance for filling up the machine. The cost would, therefore, be £20 rental + 100 x 1.25p for ink + 100 x £2.36 for the actual postage = £257.25, and a saving therefore of £12.75.

This probably wouldn't be worth the hassle and commitment of signing up for a franking machine.

On the other hand, if her business increases to 200 products per month, the cost for stamps would be £540 compared with £494.50 for franking – so the saving is now £45.50 per month or £546 per year.

For heavier products, the difference mounts up much more quickly.

Why bother?
You may be wondering if it's worth the effort, given that you will usually charge your customers for postage. Well, you won't be surprised to hear that the less you charge for postage, the more likely customers are to buy! So you owe it to your business to keep these costs down to as low a level as possible.

COURIERS
Royal Mail is our preferred method for small items and where the customer wants express delivery. Our experience is that the First Class service is pretty good these days and, except at very high weights, cheaper than next-day couriers.

However, Royal Mail (and its courier arm ParcelForce) cannot compete when it comes to economy delivery. If your package weighs more than 1kg, it cannot be sent by second class but must use the Standard Parcels service which can take up to 5 working days to arrive (second class should arrive within 3 working days).

So, to send a 1.5kg parcel via Standard Parcels costs £5.30. Economy courier myHermes, on the other hand, charges £3.49 (£4.19 incl VAT, if you're not registered) and provides tracking and an easy(ish) to use claim service in case of problems. They also pick up from your address (unlike Royal Mail), which can save a lot of time if you'd otherwise have to drive to a Post Office

For the vast majority of our deliveries, we use either Royal Mail or myHermes and experience very few problems indeed. Our customers get the lowest possible price, whatever the weight of their package, and, in most cases, we're able to track the parcel via the myHermes online system. For very heavy orders, we'll occasionally book a next-day courier – this is best done using an agent such as Parcels2Go.com.

Let Amazon do it

There's another option. If it suits your particular products, you could sell them via Amazon. The benefit of this approach is that not only are your products present on one of the biggest online shops in the world but Amazon handles payment processing and sends you the cash every two weeks.

You can also take this one step further and sign up for the Fulfilled By Amazon (FBA) programme. In brief, you send your products to one of Amazon's warehouses and, when a customer orders it, Amazon ships it with no involvement from you. They also handle all customer service, chasing the couriers if necessary.

This costs money, of course, but many customers like shopping at Amazon because they already have an account with them and can often take advantage of free shipping – so you end up selling more.

We use FBA for a limited range of our products – this comes into its own in December when less organised shoppers flood onto Amazon in search of Christmas gifts that they can rely on to be delivered in time. Our responsibility is to get enough stock up there to satisfy demand but, aside from extra sales, we're also able to close our online shop a week before Christmas whilst Amazon continues to sell our products.

Many people base their entire business around the Amazon platform – take a look at what's involved by going to **http://scrib.me/ycbFBAmz** (or **www.yourcraftbusiness.co.uk**)

BEING PAID

There's no point running a business if you can't accept money from willing customers! If you ask your bank about this, they'll start talking about Merchant Accounts and such like – and if you don't yet have a trading history they'll wave you away.

Fortunately, there are a number of very simple ways to accept payments, whether you're trading online or face to face.

ONLINE PAYMENTS

There are a range of services available to allow you to take payments online. First and foremost, you should only sign up with a reputable firm – one you've heard of or used yourself as a buyer online. You need to ask the following questions of any prospective payment provider:

- **What payment forms do you accept?** Make sure these include both Visa and Mastercard at a minimum

- **How much do they charge?** Some payment providers charge a monthly fee but almost all charge a fixed price per transaction plus a percentage. As it happens, this is pretty standard at 3.4% of the transaction plus 20p for most of the main services.

- **How quickly do they pay you?** Some payment providers remit your balance on a regular basis, with others you manually transfer. The latter is preferable because you get to control your cashflow.

- **Do they hold onto a balance?** Some payment providers hold back a percentage of your balance in case of credit card chargebacks. This will probably vary depending on your particular business.

One final thing to consider – does your shopping cart support it? Most carts will support the services listed below.

PAYPAL

Familiar to us all, Paypal is a huge company – it's owned by eBay and processed over $7 billion-worth of transactions in 2009. It's also one of the easiest to get set up with.

PAYPAL WEB PAYMENTS STANDARD

This is the service most businesses begin with. PWPS allows you to embed buttons in your website to take payments as well as integrating nicely with most shopping carts. When your customer comes to pay, they are taken to the Paypal site – they can pay using either a plastic card or an existing Paypal account.

PAYPAL WEB PAYMENTS PRO

The main practical difference between this and the PWPS is that you embed the plastic card processing within your site (from the customer's point of view) rather than sending them off to the Paypal site. This feels more professional to the customer and slightly reduces the steps needed to process a transaction.

However, PWPP costs £20 per month. MakingYourOwnCandles used PWPS to start with, switching quickly to PWPP and experiencing a significant increase in conversions so it made sense for us. As a rule of thumb, once you start processing more than £1,000 per month in transactions through PWPS, it's time to consider upgrading.

PWPP also offers other features which might prove useful to business that wish to process telephone or face to face orders as well as those taken online.

Find out about both services at **https://www.paypal-business.co.uk/**

GOOGLE WALLET

Formerly known as Google Checkout, Wallet is Google's equivalent to Paypal. Unlike Paypal, Google Wallet automatically remits your payments every two weeks (after an initial probationary period). Its main benefits are that it's easy to set up and many millions of people have Google Wallet accounts set up as they're required to purchase apps, movies and books via Google Play (primarily via Android smartphones and tablets).

Find out more at **http://www.google.com/wallet/merchants.html**

NOCHEX

Nochex is a UK-based payment processor that allows you to take plastic cards with the minimum of fuss. You probably haven't heard of it, but I've been using them successfully since 2005 and, whilst they're pretty unsexy, they do a good job. You may have to keep a reserve balance in hand but otherwise you can transfer your funds over whenever you wish.

This is a good one to try out, especially if you're only operating online.

Find out more at **www.nochex.com**

AMAZON PAYMENTS

This system allows customers to pay on your website using their existing Amazon account details. If your audience is likely to include lots of people like this, and your shopping cart supports it, this can be an excellent additional option. Bear in mind that Amazon remits every two weeks and may keep a balance in reserve.

For more information: **https://payments.amazon.co.uk/business/**

FACE TO FACE PAYMENTS

A few years ago, small businesspeople selling directly to customers face to face were mainly limited to cash and cheque. The problem with the first of these is the hassle and security issues, and with the second the hassle of having to pay them in and the fact that cheque guarantee cards no longer exist.[1]

Fortunately, technology comes to our rescue again. This is a rapidly advancing area and, over the next year, I expect to see several schemes launching in the UK that involve plugging tiny card readers into your smartphone (the original innovator in the US was Square). The first fully featured service is likely to be PayPal Here but since, at the time of writing, it had not been launched, I don't list it here.

PAYPAL VIRTUAL TERMINAL

This system, part of Paypal Web Payments Pro, essentially turns your laptop into a payment machine. Virtual Terminal allows you to take payment over the phone, by post or face to face. You would take your laptop (making sure you had some way to connect to the internet – a broadband dongle for example) and type in the customer's card details in their presence. The money is instantly transferred and you can then hand the customer their goods – it's a good idea to get a signed receipt if the value is above a level you're comfortable with, just in case they contact Paypal and dispute the transaction. Whilst a little clunky, this system works well and is well established.

Find out more at **http://scrib.me/ycbVT**

---

[1] The Cheque Guarantee Scheme was closed on 30th June 2011.

SysPay

SysPay uses a combination of a smartphone app and a PinPad terminal. You type a description and amount into your smartphone and this connects to the terminal. The customer inserts their card, types in their pin number and the transfer is made. To the customer this feels exactly like a standard card-reader transaction which is reassuring. You get the benefit of this without the big expense of standard equipment.

Find out more at https://www.syspay.com/

iZettle

The first of the Square-a-like services to launch in the UK, iZettle provides you with a tiny card reader to attach to your smartphone. The service works well enough but, at the time of writing, it only supported Mastercard – not Visa.

https://www.izettle.com/gb

CHAPTER 9: YOUR MARKETPLACE

Where do you intend to sell your goods? Most crafters choose more than one outlet for their talents – whether that's attending the odd craft fair to supplement the sales from their online shop or setting up a simple web shopping cart to back up their 'real world' sales.

In this chapter, I'm going to cover the main craft marketplaces but this isn't a book about Etsy, eBay or, indeed, craft fairs – it's a book about business and if you want detail on how to set up your Folksy shop, for example, there are plenty of other guides that cover this.

You have four main options for selling your wares:

1   By using an online marketplace

2   Through your own website

3   Selling to customers face to face

4   Selling through other retailers

ONLINE MARKETPLACES

FIRST PRINCIPLES

Whichever online platform you use, the basic principles are exactly the same so I'm going to cover them upfront.

1: CHOOSE THE RIGHT PRODUCT

We've spent a lot of time refining our product during this book because everything depends on it. Customers of crafters don't expect machine-like perfection but rather high, hand-made quality. You need to strike a balance between exceptional quality and your ability to create your products quickly enough for your business. Sometimes this means adapting an item slightly – even small changes to your process can mount up when repeated time and time again.

Generally speaking, you should choose one marketplace to begin with and get it right before expanding into another. This is partly because there simply aren't enough hours in the day to be juggling more balls than necessary but it's mainly because the lessons you learn as you become profitable in one market can be applied to others. So, setting up your first shop takes a lot of time, making it profitable will also take time – but the next one will be quicker.

You shouldn't necessarily use the same range of products across each market – it depends very much on the audience. Customers of Amazon are different from those of eBay and both are very different from Folksy customers. It not only costs more (in many cases) to list multiple products, it also dilutes your brand and makes it less likely the people that use a particular marketplace will buy from you.

For example, if you're a soap maker you might decide that Folksy customers are more likely to buy supplies for soap making rather than finished products so you put together kits and materials for those customers.[1] Amazon customers, on the other hand, are more likely to want something that looks "retail" whether that's a kit or a pack of soap.

---

[1]   I'm not saying this is true of Folksy customers – you would need to investigate – but it serves as an example

2: TAKE GOOD PHOTOS

It goes without saying that you must upload photographs of your products – but quality is, as usual, much more important than quantity.

Quality, when it comes to product shots, comes down to the following:

Camera

You don't need an expensive SLR to take product shots (although if you have one, and know how to use it properly, so much the better). For most craft products, what matters is your camera's ability to take close-up pictures. This is known as "macro" photography and if you're in the market for a camera, it's worth looking at reviews to see if it's considered good at this. Macro shots mean getting close in to the product, with the effect that the background is out of focus (it depends on the lens and the distance the object is from the camera).

If you have an SLR, this same effect is achieved by shooting from some distance with the lens on maximum zoom. This reduces the "depth of field" and means that anything behind the product is blurred.

Many smartphones now have cameras that are usable for product photography – including the iPhone5 and Samsung Galaxy S2 and S3 but a decent compact digital camera will give better results. The Nikon Coolpix S9100 (there's a link at www.yourcraftbusiness.co.uk) is a good choice. Bear in mind that it's not just about megapixels – once you get above 8 megapixels the practical difference is next to zero (unless you intend to make A2 sized posters from your shots) – what matters is the quality of the lens, sensor and software.

If at all possible, mount the camera on a tripod. That way, not only do you get sharp photos but it makes it easy to get the position right at the beginning and then make minor adjustments to the product and its background without having to reposition the camera again.

Lights

Good lighting is absolutely essential. Whilst modern cameras, and smartphones, can cope with low light conditions, the end result is often a grainy or smudgy photo.

The good news is that the best light for most situations is natural light so taking your products out into the garden on a sunny day means you can get lots of shots done in a short time. If the sun is low in the sky, shadows might be a problem – in that case the best approach is usually to find a place where the sun isn't shining directly on the object. If that isn't possible you can cover a sheet of cardboard with zinc foil and hold it on the opposite side of the product to the sun, directing the reflected light to cancel out the shadow.

If you decide to shoot indoors, try to use halogen lights with a bright white colour – standard incandescent bulbs tend to have a yellowish cast. Position them so that they don't shine directly onto the product but light up the area around it.

Background
There are two schools of thought on this. The first is that photos should be shot against a neutral background (white, grey or black depending on your product). Done well, photos like this look as though they've been shot in a studio giving an extra sense of professionalism. It also ensures that your item is the main focus of the photo.

However, achieving a good "studio-style" shot can be tricky and is best achieved with a light-box set. This consists of a cube-shaped pop-up tent with an open front, some lights and, usually, a camera stand. The product is placed inside the tent, the lights to either side and the camera is pointed through the hole at the front. With small products this can work very well indeed.

The other popular option is to deliberately choose an appropriate background for each product. In the case of a candle intended for use in the bath, for example, the shot could be of the candle on the side of the tub or against some bath tiles. Jewellery could be modelled by a human being (even if only a neck or hand are visible) rather than on a sterile background.

I've changed my point of view over time and I now tend to prefer this more naturalistic approach. We are, after all, talking about hand made products. On the other hand, the studio approach is more efficient if you have lots of products to shoot in one go as you can set everything up and simply replace the items for the next shot very quickly.

If you're short on time and have a lot of products, then the studio option is probably the best bet since, even if it does result in "sterile" photos, they will at least be clear and professional. Taking lots of naturalistic shots is more time consuming as it usually involves changing sets and locations more often but the end results are often better.

There's one final advantage of this more natural approach: your customers get a much better sense of how large the item is as they're able to compare it against a familiar background.

It depends on your audience – which type of shot do you think they'd prefer? One thing is certain, either of these is better than hastily taken, low quality photos – these will do nothing other than undermine you and your product in the minds of your customers.

Quality rather than quantity

How many photos? The short answer is "enough". Many of the marketplace platforms charge you per photo (although the first is usually free) and you should always have at least two – a shot of the product as a whole and then a closer, more detailed shot. Upload these photos in high quality as this way the system you use will usually offer a "zoom in" view so the customer can examine your product in more detail.

When selling online, potential customers can't pick up, feel or smell your product. You're left with sight as the only sense – you'd better take every opportunity to make the most of it if you're to convert browsers into buyers.

3: TELL THEM ALL ABOUT IT

How many times have you been browsing for something on eBay only to be put off by the poor quality of the description? Here are three classic mistakes you must avoid:

Lack of detail

You know your product inside out – tell your potential customer everything they could possibly want to know. What is it made of? What should it be used for? How does it feel or smell? Are there any usage instructions?

Expecting customers to guess what they're getting is crazy – and to the customer it appears you're being lazy or dismissive. It is almost impossible to add too much detail so if in doubt add it in.

"No time wasters"

How does seeing "re-listed due to time wasters" or "negative feedback will be left if you don't pay quickly" make you feel about the shop-owner? To me, it feels as though he or she believes they're doing me a favour by listing the item. I wouldn't expect to get good customer service from this person and I almost certainly wouldn't buy from them.

Yes, there are a small number of time-wasters but don't poison the well for everyone else – in my experience the vast majority of craft customers are decent folk.

Unclear postage

If at all possible, especially on eBay, give free postage. Products that have free shipping appear higher in the eBay search than identical products that don't so your item will be seen by more people. In truth, we all know that the cost of postage is added to the product price but people like feeling they're seeing the full price on eBay and other platforms.

If you ship internationally, then for heaven's sake make the effort to set the postage up for this. As you work it out on one product, write it down so that the work's already done for a later one. The customer must be able to buy from you without having to email you first – otherwise they'll simply find another seller who has made the effort.

And finally, make sure you despatch quickly – and include this promise in your copy. Fast despatch of a nicely packaged product with a hand written note is a great way to get the sort of excellent feedback that will encourage others to buy from you.

EBAY

A lot of people start selling their crafts through eBay and it's certainly easy enough to get up and running.

Whilst you can sell single items, this is really aimed at individuals. You're setting up in business, so you should create an eBay shop of your own. There is a cost for this (around £20 per month at the time of writing) but you get discounts on various listing fees along with various tools to manage your shop.

The main benefit of setting up an eBay shop, however, is that customers are more likely to see you as a proper business and are therefore more likely to buy. You can brand the shop with your logo, colour scheme and copy so that if a customer clicks on the link contained in any product listing, they'll see your entire stock. This makes it more likely they'll make additional purchases from you or, if the original product wasn't quite what they wanted, that they'll by an alternative from you rather than a competitor.

It's usually best to list your products as "buy it now" rather than auction items, otherwise you run the risk of selling them for less than they cost to make. Customers subconsciously associated a "buy it now" listing as being more professional and shop-like in any case.

Our experience was that eBay customers tend to be much more price conscious than visitors to our website. Being price conscious means they're looking for the lowest possible price rather than the best value and our business is focused on the latter. You may find that your audience is entirely different – that's why it's important to experiment with different platforms.

The trick is to spend just long enough building and running your shop to work out whether it's for you and your business. This can be a difficult balancing act – bail out too early and you'll miss out on a potentially lucrative way of selling your products, hold on too long and you could be throwing good money and time after bad.

We closed our shop after a few months when we judged that the effort required to run it wasn't worth the money it generated – especially compared to our own website.

AMAZON MARKETPLACE

Amazon has a number of ways you can take advantage of it. As with eBay, you can sell individual items but most businesses will need to sign up for the Pro Merchant account (£25 per month + VAT). The fee structure is such that if you sell more than around 30 items per month on Amazon, it's cheaper to be a Pro Merchant but I'd recommend going pro from the beginning as it includes a professional control panel and tools that help you manage your stock.

By signing up as a Pro merchant you also get a shop-front on Amazon so that any customer finding you through one of your products can see your whole range by clicking your shop name. If you see your product being used as a gift, then Amazon is a good place to be – especially in the pre-Christmas frenzy as customers seek to do all their shopping through one service.

As I mentioned earlier, we've signed up for the Fulfilled by Amazon service which, by and large, is working well. By using this service, our products show up as "Sold by MakingYourOwnCandles and Fulfilled by Amazon". This means they get the reassurance of Amazon's pretty reliable delivery service, excellent customer service and free delivery. None of this impacts on us as we don't pay directly for it – Amazon simply deducts the appropriate fee from the amount it sends us. This meant that we adjusted our prices somewhat to ensure both that our profit margin was maintained and that customers visiting our site get the best deal.

ETSY AND FOLKSY

Essentially, these marketplaces work the same way – with Folksy focusing on the UK and Etsy covering both this country and the international market. Everything I've said about eBay and Amazon applies here – especially the importance of setting up your own shop.

Think carefully about whether your audience is likely to shop using either of these platforms. For more esoteric crafts, they're likely to be a good choice but for mainstream products you'll probably find that eBay or Amazon generate more sales. There's no harm in experimenting with an Etsy or Folksy site – just be aware that there are listing fees and, in the case of Etsy at least, a renewal fee.

SELLING FACE TO FACE

For some people, the idea of attempting to sell their products to real live customers face to face fills them with horror. Visions of pushy salespeople and difficult to please patrons haunt their worst nightmares. But selling craft products shouldn't be like that and there's nothing like the thrill of a happy customer handing over real money for your product. It feels great!!

LIVE EVENTS

This category includes fetes, exhibitions and jumble sales but let's call them all "craft fairs" for the sake of convenience.

Depending on your personality, craft fairs can be exciting or frightening but, either way, they will **certainly** be hard work. Think about it – you're essentially setting up and dismantling a shop in one day. This almost always means an early start and a late finish.

Before you book a pitch at a craft fair or similar event, make sure you have the answers to these questions:

1: How much is a pitch?
Remember that this represents a fixed cost – so it'll end up being deducted from your profit whether you sell more than you could imagine, or hardly anything.

2: How many people will be there?
This is the critical number. At least at the beginning, you should only attend craft fairs with an established track record. Ask how many people visited the fair at the equivalent event last year. You can now see the pitch fee in context – paying £10 for a 500 passers-by is a much worse deal than paying £30 for 5,000!

3: What do I need to bring?
Some craft fairs provide everything and set it all up for you – all you need to do is turn up with your products and lay them out (and, of course, pack the unsold products away at the end). Often, however, you'll be asked to bring your own tables and, especially for outside events, you'll also need to provide your own gazebo.

If the organisers provide the tables, find out what size they are so you can plan how you're going to lay your stock out at home.

4: What are the timings?

You need to know when the craft fair starts and ends but the two most important times (for you) are: when should you turn up and when can you leave. Larger craft fairs, particularly those taking place outside, will sometimes book you a slot so that you can drive down to the pitch and unload but, in every case, you will need to be there some time before the doors open.

More surprisingly, most craft fairs also have a rule about when you can leave. They don't want the place to be deserted early so, even if you've sold your entire stock, you are supposed to wait until closing time. This might seem particularly depressing if sales aren't going well but, to be honest, you should give it the full day in any case.

5: Insurance

You will often be asked to produce your public liability insurance certificate although, in some cases, this will be covered by the venue

HOW MUCH STOCK?

This is the single most commonly asked question about craft fairs. Well, having got the information above, you know two things. Firstly, how many people are visiting the fair and secondly how big your table is.

First and foremost you must make enough stock to fill your table up!

Beyond that, it's a case of looking at the number of people predicted to attend and taking a punt. If the event is likely to attract 5,000 people, you're going to need more stock than the local church bazaar!

I recommend that you always err on the side of making too much rather than too little. Be confident – after all you'll be able to sell any remaining stock through other channels after the fair in any case.

As for the stock itself, you should include a fairly wide range of your products. This should include some low price items – broadly speaking the lower the price, the more of them you want. And yes, I know I've been banging on about creating premium products and that is, indeed, where your main effort should lie. However, much of the task at a craft fair is to create a buzz around your stall and there's no better way to do this than by having some "bargains". There may not be massive profit in each of these sales but other buyers are attracted to your stall by the sight of people buying and *those customers might buy a premium item.*

One option is to offer damaged products – for example miscast candles or soaps, jams with misprinted labels or near their sell-by dates, or out of season products. Another option is to offer samplers – a tiny roll-up beeswax sheet candle that costs you 20p but sells for £1 for example.

This is one way in which craft fairs differ from selling online. People will find your Etsy shop by searching in Google, for example, whereas at a craft fair your first job is to attract attention. Creating activity around your stall is a great way of doing this.

Another option is to offer demonstrations of your craft. For example, rather than selling roll-up candles, you could get passers-by to make candles themselves. Alternatively, you could be making objects during the fair – although this only works for certain crafts.

You also need to think about how you're going to mark prices. This depends very much on the type of craft – but if you have several products at the same price, you could use a folded "tent" of cardboard. Generally speaking, however, price everything individually and clearly unless you can group them into containers. **People hate asking how much something costs!**

CRAFT FAIR TIPS

Pick a local one
For your first fair, you should go local. This is partly so that you can visit it before you book a table but also because you don't want to have to travel too far for your first fair.

Display like a pro
Create a colourful display that shows off your products to their best. Cover the table with a colourful cloth and slide box files underneath to create height at the back – this looks much, much better than a flat display. Now, fill up the space so that it's brimming with product. For your first few craft fairs, it's worth practising this at home.

Turn up early!
Do not be in a rush, especially the first time. Whenever you do anything unfamiliar, it takes extra time and you want your display to be as attractive as those of the old hands either side of you.

Take a partner
Don't do this alone! If you do, you'll end up tied to the table for the whole day. Also bear in mind that you can only serve one customer at a time, so when it gets busy you might be losing business. Your partner in crime needn't be a crafter themselves, they just need to be someone who can count out change and who you can trust to look after the stall while you run off to the loo.

Have plenty of change!
You don't want to have to turn buyers away because you can't change their money! In a perfect world, you'd have a portable card reader so you could take cash or Paypal's Virtual Terminal but that's not realistic for your first craft fair. So, take plenty of change – you can always pay it back into the bank after the fair's over.

Think about your table layout
If you only have one table, or they're laid out for you by the organisers then ignore this. If you are using multiple tables, however, you will need to think about how you organise them.

Generally speaking an "n" shape is ideal. In other words, the customers walk "into" an area bounded by three sides. You sit or stand behind the one at the top of the "n". This way, customers can look at all your products without feeling they're too close to you (people don't like to feel they're being watched!) and they follow a natural flow around each of the three sides.

You could also try a "u" shape with one or more tables along the walkway. This way, customers walk around the outside and you stand inside the u. The advantage of this shape is that there's more room for customers to move, and you're easily able to serve anyone. Bear in mind, however, that if you're outside under a gazebo, your customers might get wet if it rains – if the weather looks at all iffy, you should use the n shape.

Essential supplies
A few other things you mustn't forget (in addition to your stock, table cloth and box files for height)

- Something to sit on

- Something to pack purchases in

- Something to record purchases on as they're made (a clipboard with a hand drawn table on lined paper would do)

- A receipt book – some customers will want one

- Bum bag for your cash

- A stack of business cards or leaflets advertising where people can buy more of your stuff – this is especially important as Christmas approaches

- If you're outside, tarpaulins to cover everything in case of rain

- Water

- Food – especially chocolate!!

- A flask of tea or coffee

- A smile.

SELLING SKILLS

You don't need any! Contrary to popular belief (and the belief of retailers and car dealers everywhere) selling is about making a human connection and **listening**.

If you are friendly and prepared to chat with people, then the worst that can happen is you'll have an enjoyable day being sociable (and that, in itself, can make a nice change!). What you'll find, however, is that by not trying to sell, you will actually sell.

What if someone tries to haggle? Well, this is where the fact that you have a very good grasp on your true product cost and the margin comes in. If you follow the TPC+75% approach, you know that if you give the customer, say, a 10% discount you're actually reducing your profit by more than 20%[1]. So, just bear that in mind when you're negotiating and remember to have confidence in your product. If you've spent £10 making an item that's on sale for £17.50 and your customer wants a discount that reduces your £7.50 profit down to £5 does that feel fair or not? You may decide it does but, personally, I wouldn't have it. If the customer wants your item, they should pay the ticket price unless there's a very good reason otherwise. Your products are worth it!!!

---

[1]   Say the TPC is £10, the margin is £7.50 and the sale price £17.50. The customer asks for £1.75 discount (10%). £1.75 is 23% of your £7.50 profit (not 10%)

TOP TIPS FOR CRAFT-FAIRS

Elaine from Littlecote Soap Co, has a lot of experience at craft-fairs – here are her top tips

GET A SIGN!

At a craft show, one of the biggest mistake that people make is not having a sign to say what they are selling. It might be abundantly clear to you that your candles made in tea cups are indeed candles, but make sure that people can instantly identify what you sell. People have just a few seconds to view your stall and make up their mind whether to approach you or not. Let people know what your USP is (unique selling point – the thing that makes you different from all the rest). Tell the customer clearly exactly what you do and why you are great at it. Have a picture of yourself at the potting wheel, or making your jewellery, as pictures speak louder than words.

PRESENTATION IS VITAL

Cover your table with appropriate fabric for your product, make sure that it is not too patterned, let the product stand out. DZD sells grocery grass by the meter, it also sells wonderful fabric that looks like Scandinavian wood – I made our "wood" fabric to fit our craft table and many people actually think it is real wood. Alternatively use hessian which is cheap and rustic looking. Use old crates, leather suitcases, old hatboxes etc. to display your products.

Height is important. Make sure that your products are eye level, the less the customer has to work to view your products, the easier it will sell.

PRICE TAGS

Clearly display the prices. People will rarely ask how much a product is if it doesn't have a price and will walk on by, so make sure that every single item is clearly marked.

OFFERS

Do a show offer. People love a bargain and you want them to buy your product NOW at the show before they go home and forget about you. Tell people that the offer is only available today. People will often part with £5 or £10 quite easily at a show.

YOU'RE NOT SELLING CARS

"Sell" your products, but don't be too pushy. A hard sell will often put off a customer, some don't even like being talked to at all as they think you are going to give them a hard sell. Smile at each customer and say "hello" or "good morning". If their feet turn inwards towards your stand this means that they are interested, so you can then say to them "have you seen us before" or "did you know that our products are local" etc.

BE HAPPY!

If you are having a bad or slow sale and people are not purchasing, refrain from sitting on your chair looking glum as it is very unlikely that you will sell anything. It might alert customers to the fact that you are having a bad show and they may wonder why your product is not selling. Try and remain cheerful and remember that it is not just what you sell at a show, use it as an advertising opportunity to direct more people to your website or blog. Use the opportunity to give away as many leaflets or business cards as you can.

PROMOTE YOURSELF

Leaflets are cheap to produce with Vistaprint or other online printing companies. This can make a nice addition to the sale of your product if there are details and pictures of how and where your product is made. Make sure that your contact details or website are on all literature, business cards, and on your product so that people can easily re-purchase.

BE NICE

Be nice to the other stall holders and the organisers. Try not to get too uptight about people invading your space or getting in your way. If you are easy to work with, other crafters, and the organisers, will recommend your products to others, and you are more than likely to be asked back again next time to the show and to other shows.

SELLING IN SHOPS

Despite gloomy times overall, there are plenty of places selling craft items. Whilst, at this stage, it's probably a little ambitious to imagine your product is going to appear on the shelves of John Lewis any time soon, there are alternatives.

Garden centres are a prime candidate. They sell a wide range of high margin items, including craft products. Have a stroll round your local garden centres and take a look at what they stock. Taking candles as an example, you'll notice that most of their products are firmly in the premium price bracket!

Most garden centres are run by a local manager who has at least some power to stock locally made products. Once you've worked out whether your product will fit with them (don't expect them to create a whole new section for you) then make an appointment to see the manager, taking along some of the stock you think would be suitable.

Remember that packaging is essential in this case – the products need to be able to withstand handling by customers. The retailer may say that your product needs a barcode so that they can add it to their systems. Don't worry about this, it's very easy to do – I use http://www.barcode1.co.uk/ . You can buy a barcode for around £25 and it's sent as an image file which you can print out or even type into a Dymo printer and stick to the box.

Sale or return

You're unlikely to be able to persuade the manager to buy your products outright (at least to start with), even at a heavy discount. They're much more likely to agree to a sale or return arrangement whereby you provide stock for no upfront fee – this stock is agreed and signed for by the garden centre and you then return periodically to replenish stock and record sales. You then invoice the garden centre for those sales.

You will need to agree a price for each product – this will be well below the retail price because the whole point of the exercise (from the point of view of the manager) is for the garden centre to make money. As a guide, the garden centre or gift shop will want to put a £25 price ticket on a product you sell to them for £10 and this is where making premium products really pays off – after all if your product doesn't look like it's worth £25, they won't stock it. A £10 product at TCP + 75% means you make a profit of around £4.50.

This is one reason that garden centres are so expensive to buy gifts from. Think about it – if you're buying a product online, you expect it to be cheaper than in a shop, not least because it's much cheaper to provide a product on a website than it is in a retailer with salaries and rent to pay.

Make your price changes before you see the manager – that way you'll know what the profit for you will be right from the start.

One final note. You probably shouldn't approach a retailer until you have been selling your products for a few months using other channels. This gives you time to tweak your products and to identify which are your best sellers. It also means you can go into the meeting with some real facts and figures rather than just guesswork. Finally, having sold some of your products and received excellent customer feedback, you will be much more confident about approaching a retailer and seeing your products on the shelf alongside those from big established businesses.

CHAPTER 10: YOU AND YOUR WEBSITE

We covered selling your products using online marketplaces, at face to face events and through retailers in the last chapter but, whatever ways you choose to sell, you need a website.

WHY YOU **MUST** HAVE A WEBSITE

Whether or not you intend to sell products directly from your own site, you must have a website.

Firstly, your website is your digital business card. The first thing potential customers do when they hear about you is look you up online and they immediately form an opinion of you. Having a website also makes it possible for people to find you by searching online. If you don't have a site, you're effectively invisible outside of any marketplaces you use.

Having a website gives you credibility – potential customers often feel that if you've made the effort (and, in their view, spent the money) to have a site built, that indicates you're a serious business. You can further enhance your credibility by writing expert articles about your craft – this also brings in free traffic from the search engines.

To sell, you need to be visible- a website is a cheap and very effective form of marketing even if you don't sell from it directly.

Most new craft businesses *will* sell their products from their website, however. The critical decision to make at the beginning is whether the website will be the **primary** shopfront or whether it's there to supplement a main income generated elsewhere (at craft fairs or via eBay or whatever).

If you intend to sell primarily through your site then you should consider a hosted ecommerce platform. What does this mean? Well, a hosted service is one that includes its own web space so you haven't got to provide that yourself. Ecommerce is the name given to selling online.

Two of the best ecommerce packages are BigCommerce (www.bigcommerce.com) and Volusion (www.volusion.com). Each offers free trials so there's no harm in trying out both of them to see which you prefer. MakingYourOwnCandles.co.uk uses BigCommerce and it's our recommended platform.[1]

[1]   On the other hand EKMPowershop and Actinic Online should, in my view, be avoided at all costs. EKM, in particular, is an awful product in my experience. Some people seem to like it, but I can only imagine they must never have experienced Volusion or BigCommerce.

Hosted eCommerce

So, how does it work? Essentially what you're getting is a shop system with two sides: the shop-front that your customers see and the back-office that you use. Both BigCommerce and Volusion come with a good range of shop designs which you can customise – although it's fair to say that the more radical customisations need some web design and development skills.

There's a certain amount of setup needed when you first start your trial shop but this is pretty straightforward as both systems provide a step-by-step checklist. Once the design looks as you want it, you then add the details of whichever payment processing method you've chosen, followed by shipping settings. BigCommerce includes a live connection to the Royal Mail servers which means you can have it generate shipping quotes on the fly but this proved less useful than you might imagine for us and we ended up creating a manual postage table which we update each time the postage rises.

Adding products is also pretty simple – roughly similar to the process for creating eBay or Amazon listings – and you can also keep track of quantities, offer bulk discounts and even embed videos within the product pages. All of this is done via a point and click interface, very simple indeed.

The real strength of a fully-featured ecommerce system, however, is the sophisticated back-office functionality. For example, both BigCommerce and Volusion offer excellent order tracking and management, along with built-in methods to communicate with customers about their order. They also allow you to add very complex options across a whole range of products very simply – for example allowing you to ask the customer for colour and size information and to adjust the price accordingly.

If your main focus is selling from your site, then I strongly recommend going for one of these services from the start as switching ecommerce packages later is difficult and time consuming. It doesn't matter if you don't have very many products to start with – we had only four – you can usually find variations that will make it appear that you have a lot more, until you complete your range.

One final point: there are a number of open source free ecommerce packages out there- the best being PrestaShop and osCommerce. You might consider these if you have technical expertise of your own or can rely on someone but, as they need to be hosted on your own site, you need to factor in the cost of providing that hosting. Once you've done that, and taking into account that they're not as sophisticated as BigCommerce and Volusion, it's rarely worth the bother and risk.

BUSINESS WEBSITE

If you don't intend to sell online, but want a website to support your business then you have a number of choices.

Ideally, you'd have the budget to engage a designer to create a professional website. If so, then make certain you've seen the quality of their work beforehand – lots of people call themselves designers without necessarily having any design expertise at all. On the other hand, there are some very good designers out there for a reasonable price.

Another option is to post a project at 99designs.co.uk. That way you can get a design made which a technically competent developer could use to create your site (or include the development of the site in the quote).

If you can't afford a quality designer then don't hire at all – believe me a site designed by an amateur is worse than no site at all. Fortunately you still have options.

Option 1: Plug and play

The first option is to sign up for an all-in-one business package. These packages are similar to the ecommerce services above in that they have a back-end management side that you use to set up and run the site, and a front-end that customers see. They're also similar in that they include hosting within the monthly subscription.

Internet host 1&1 offers their MyWebsite package but my current favourite is Heart Internet's SiteDesigner Pro (links to both are at www.yourcraftbusiness.co.uk). In both cases, you can choose from a range of templates suited to businesses – including some that are appropriate for craft shops. You edit the site from your browser and changes are visible immediately. If you have no technical expertise, these services represent the simplest way to get a good quality website up and running with the minimum of fuss.

Warning

Type "create a website" into Google and a number of services will appear including Wix and Moonfruit. Whilst these services can be used to create good quality websites, they still rely heavily on a technology called Flash. Without getting into too much detail, if your site is built using Flash almost all mobile devices will be unable to use it **and** it becomes essentially invisible to Google when it comes to indexing it.

If you choose to try out one of these services, ask them whether their sites use Flash and, if so, move along to the next. Neither MyWebsite by 1&1 nor SiteDesigner Pro uses Flash.

Option 2: WordPress

WordPress began life as a blogging platform but its technology now powers around 15% of all the websites in the world – including plenty of the websites you visit. Unlike SiteBuilder or MyWebsite, the focus of WordPress is to supply a scaffold that includes excellent site management software – you add a design to suit.

WordPress is a software package that you install on your server. Don't panic, however, because Heart Internet (amongst others) includes a one-click install of WordPress with their business hosting packages. So, in this case, you'd buy your domain name (web address), add on the Home Pro hosting package as part of the process and, once done, double click the icon to set up WordPress. This automatically creates your website and adds a plain, default look to it.

If you like punishing yourself, you can now go into WordPress and manually alter its appearance to suit. Sensible human beings, on the other hand, will install a "theme" to give their site a design they like. This is done very simply, within the WordPress control panel in your browser and you can try as many as you like before settling on one.

Most are entirely free of charge, and even those that do cost money are very cheap – much cheaper than hiring a designer.

This approach is the one I prefer as you end up with the design you want and you have a system that's very flexible. For example, you can very easily add "plugins" to WordPress to add extra features. Perhaps you want to add a contact form, for instance – with a plugin it's a matter of a few minutes work, and costs nothing (usually).

To summarise – if you have no interest whatsoever in getting into the nitty gritty of maintaining a website, you can't afford to hire someone to help you and you don't have a willing family member you can co-opt, I suggest the 1&1 or Heart Internet products. Otherwise, for a more expandable, flexible site that's adaptable to almost any circumstance, choose WordPress

Option 3: Plug in and sell

If your website is going to be your primary online shop then, in most cases, it's best to go with a fully featured ecommerce package such as BigCommerce. However, if your range is very small or you're also selling elsewhere but want to offer your goods on your site, there's another option.

Heart Internet's SiteDesigner Pro includes an optional shopping cart but the most flexible option is, again, likely to be WordPress. There are a number of plugins you can install that add shopping cart functionality to your WordPress site. Depending on the particular plugin, this can range from a simple PayPal integration to a fully-featured back-office system. A plugin called "WP e-commerce" is probably the place to start as it offers a free version along with various low-priced enhancements depending on what you require.

Case Study: www.MakingYourOwnCandles.co.uk

In our case, we based our shop on BigCommerce. Since originally setting it up, we completely changed our design at the start of 2012 – a process that only took a few hours. Designs are changed by choosing from the list of available themes and then editing this to suit if necessary.

We've created additional pages within BigCommerce, for example for our terms and conditions and "about us" information.

We also created a blog: MakingYourOwnCandlesBlog.co.uk which contains tips and projects for candle makers. This contains links to the main shop which means we not only get traffic from the site but it also improves the shop's ranking on Google.

Case Study: www.sayitwithbrownies.co.uk

How did you have your website developed?

*"My website was developed by the same marketing agency who created the Say It With Brownies branding and packaging designs (**www.peekaboodesign.co.uk**). I knew I wanted the concept of choosing your gift packaging message and choosing your flavour of brownies, plus I wanted to be able to show customer reviews and feedback. I had a long list of wants and Peekaboo Design pretty much managed to accommodate them all. My website is based on WordPress and it is easy for me to use as orders for brownies come in. I can blog about what I'm up to, add photographs and keep track of customer reviews. It was important that the shopping process was as easy and streamlined as possible for customers. Only a professional web designer would be able to deliver a website of the quality that I knew I needed. My contribution was to take most of the photographs and to write all of the copy which I was comfortable doing."*

Case Study: www.littlecotesoap.co.uk

How did you have your website developed?

> "To start with I created my own website. This is really easy and cheap to do with companies such as 1&1 you just choose the template and upload your information and images. Make sure that your photographs are really good, if you cannot do them yourself, get a friend to do them for you as these are vital for good web sales. After a few years, we went to a professional web company as we needed more from our website. My advice would be to get a website straight away as soon as you start so that you secure your preferred website name, it also takes the search engines to realise that you are there, but more importantly you can give our your website at craft shows so that people can re-order or see your latest products."

Your website: what to include

The bare minimum
All sites should include the following information:

What you do
In other words, a clear description of your craft and the products you create. It's all too easy for you to get so close to your business that you forget to tell customers very clearly what you're offering.

Who you are
Craft products are, by their nature, hand made and customers want to know who owns those hands! A short biography explaining how you came to take up your craft and how that led into a business helps make that connection. The internet helps the smallest of businesses compete with the big retailers and one big advantage you have, as a microbusiness, is your uniqueness and personality – make something of it.

Where your products can be purchased
If you don't sell online, then it's essential your website tells prospective customers where they can find your products. For example, all your craft fair bookings should appear on the front page so customers can clearly see where you'll be and when.

If you sell via an Etsy or eBay shop, include a prominent link to it – after all your website could become a very important traffic source. This is like directing them through the front door of a high street shop - you get first bite at the cherry.

Legal info
If you're a limited company, you must show your company number and registered address on your website.

You should also include a privacy policy and, if you sell from the site, terms and conditions. Fortunately, you can download standard versions of these documents and amend them to suit – for example from **www.simply-docs.co.uk** (I'm required to point out that you should seek independent legal advice).

The cookie monster

You may have heard of the Cookie Law and you'll almost certainly have seen websites with messages about cookies recently. This has been an almighty mess – it started out looking as though every site was going to have to include an annoying popup and has now become very vague. My understanding, from the guidance I've seen, is that for most purposes it is enough to include mention of cookies in your privacy policy – this is already included in most cases. This is because your site is not going to be storing data that can identify a person – cookies are used in WordPress for purely housekeeping purposes.

A cookie is simply a tiny text file stored on the users' computers. If someone logs into a site, for example, encrypted information is saved to the cookie because otherwise the browser would forget they're logged in when they move to another page. Cookies are also used to target advertising (ever noticed how the same adverts appear time and time again? This is because they've spotted something they think you're interested in) and it's these cookies that the law is aimed at primarily.

So, unless you intend to include advertising in your site, this is unlikely to affect you.

Cookies play an important role in ecommerce as they're used to make shopping carts function. Whichever shopping technology you use, it will include cookies – however, these are considered "essential" cookies so you don't need to get the visitor's permission to use them.

BLOG

It's inevitable that once you build a business based on your craft, you will spend more and more time making products. During this process, you'll become increasingly adept – learning new techniques, solving problems and creating novel versions of your products. These are all good topics for a blog.

Blogs were originally conceived as online diaries so, by default, they present information organised by date. However, you can also organise by topic and most blogs do this – although they'll usually present entries within a topic in date order, newest at the top.

We created a separate site (**www.makingyourowncandlesblog.co.uk**) for our blogging. This was partly because our main site is an online shop and not suited to being a blogging platform, and it's also because by having the blog separate, the links we have to the main shop more effectively boost our search engine ranking.

The blog uses WordPress, not surprisingly, and we've split our entries into various categories including Projects, Hints and Tips and recycling. MakingYourOwnCandlesBlog.co.uk gets thousands of visitors per month, all of whom are exposed to our brand – for free.

I'm not going to pretend that a blog is an essential asset. Ours certainly gets more of our attention during the (for us) quieter summer months – once peak season looms it's generally all hands to the pump. It's a long term, secondary activity but it can pay off in a big way if you commit to updating regularly.

You don't even need to create the blog yourself – you could use services such as Blogger.com (owned by Google) or WordPress.com (which is a version of WordPress which is hosted by them, so there's nothing to set up). In a perfect world, you'd have a blog on a domain name you own but if that's not something you fancy doing, a Blogger blog is much better than no blog at all.

MILESTONE 5: SORT OUT YOUR WEBSITE!

There's no putting it off any longer! You've got your products and you've decided where to sell them – you now need a website to help make this happen.

Take a look at the services I've mentioned, and perhaps others that you come across (just bear in mind that my recommendations have been tested personally by me), sign up for trials and, when you're happy you've made the right choice, get your site built.

CHAPTER 11: MARKETING YOUR BUSINESS

Newcomers to the crafting business have two secret fears. The first relates to whether they're good enough at their craft – is a customer going to take one look at your hand made product and suggest you get a job? Hopefully, if you ever had that fear, you should be over it by now. Creating a product using the process I've described makes it much more likely to fit the market you've chosen and should immunise you from doubts about its quality.

The second secret fear is that you'll open your shop and no-one will come: whether that's your Folksy shop, your own website or a stand at a craft fair. I covered fairs in the last chapter, so hopefully you're now confident that you can lay out a compelling display and have people flocking to your stand.

THE "TRAFFIC" MYTH

"Traffic" refers to visitors but it's important to always remember that what you really want is **customers**. Imagine you've set up a high street shop selling preserves and you rope in family and friends to wander the streets to drum up interest. You are very sensibly offering free cake (free cake is **always** good) as an incentive for people to visit.

One strategy would be to ask your representatives to go up to as many people as possible and tell them that there's free cake available in your shop. What do you think the result of this would be? Yes, a shop full of people eating free cake – you may even have people waiting outside unable to get in.

The second strategy would be to get your representatives to pick people from the appropriate age range (you know who your customers are likely to be, don't you?) and ask them whether they like high quality jams, chutneys and pickles. If the answer is "yes", send them along to the shop; if "no", wish them a good day.

This strategy will result in fewer people turning up to eat your cake **but** those people are much more likely to buy as they've been hand-picked as potential customers. They would also turn up under the first strategy, but would probably not find such a packed shop a good environment to inspect your wares.

"Traffic", then, is just a measure of the number of visitors. Free traffic is always good (online at least, not so much in a small shop) because even though only a small proportion of this traffic might be potential buyers, they've cost you nothing so any sales you make are a bonus. If you pay for traffic, however, you must make sure that enough of those visitors convert to buying customers to make the marketing pay for itself.

THE BRAND NEW CUSTOMER MYTH

The best customer is a repeat customer – something that many of the biggest retailers and service companies seem unable to grasp. Mobile phone companies, for example, offer attractive deals to new customers but when a contract expires, the upgrades available are poor. Their hope, presumably, is that enough people won't notice that the offer is so poor, that they'll get away with it. In my case, I change provider every two years and benefit from being a "new customer" each time.

It costs much more time and money to attract a new customer than to sell again to an existing one. In the case of the mobile phone companies, they calculate that they will make more money on my renewal if they offer me a cheap phone for my upgrade (assuming I don't notice that they're taking the mickey). My new phone provider will have spent marketing money attracting me, in many cases paid commission to an agent such as Phones4U and (in my case) TopCashBack or QuidCo which would have been better spent by my existing provider in keeping me loyal.

Fortunately for us, people who run small businesses are also consumers so we know this instinctively. Your customers, the people who've actually purchased from you, are your most precious resource – even more valuable than your product line. They have made a judgement that your product is worth buying and you're worth buying from.

Since you created a premium product, they're almost certain to be happy with it – which makes them even more valuable to you – if the overall experience of buying from you matched the quality of the product.

So, marketing first and foremost is about **keeping** customers rather than attracting them. This might seem the wrong way round but look at it this way – if you're in a sinking rowing boat, you'd better make sure the bucket doesn't leak before using it to bail out. Supplying a premium product in a premium manner and then **over-delivering** in some way, makes it much more likely that the customer will buy again.

What does "over-delivering" mean? It means adding something **unexpected** to the order – whether that's the process or the product itself.

For example:

1: Handwritten note
It costs nothing to add a handwritten note to the order, except a few seconds of your time. If the customer has shopped before, then add detail such as "I hope you enjoy this as much as the [product]". Customers like to know that they've received a little personal attention in an impersonal world.

2: Freebie
Bear in mind that the cost price to you of your products is much lower than the price you charge. Many businesspeople resist giving away a product with a list price of, for example £5 because they see it as a lost £5. The truth, however, is that the product might have cost £1.50 and you might see this as a reasonable investment in your relationship with this customer.

3: Faster-than-expected delivery
Ship it quicker than expected – but only if it's going by Royal Mail otherwise your customer might be annoyed to find a "missed you" card on the floor.

4: Money off next order
Drop a voucher into the box which entitles them to a discount next time they order, or a code to give a friend.

We also give an automatic 5% discount to every customer after their second order – they have to do nothing to activate it, it simply appears as a deduction on their shopping card when they next place an order.

5: In general
Find ways to express your appreciation in a human, genuine way. This isn't about cynical marketing techniques, we use all of the above at different times because we truly appreciate the fact that people buy stuff from us, even after three years!

DEALING WITH CAPTAIN COCKUP

On the other hand, how you deal with under-delivering is critical. Cockups do happen – sometimes you, as a human being, will make a mistake or, more often, the problem will be caused during the delivery process by your agent. The most difficult cockups to handle, however, are those committed by the customer themselves – the idea that "the customer is always right" is nonsense. A better mantra is "the customer should never lose out".

1: If you make a mistake

This is pretty simple – own up immediately. If you spot it before your customer, let them know as soon as you can and, at the same time, tell them what you're going to do about it. If they've been at all inconvenienced, add something to the order to compensate them.

2: If the delivery goes wrong

It's a fact of life that sometimes a delivery doesn't turn up, turns up late or is damaged in transit. If a customer complains that their item hasn't arrived, and the timescale they've paid for has expired, chase it up immediately with the courier and if it can't be resolved very quickly, ship a new product by the fastest method possible. Only then should you seek compensation from the courier.

If you've used a non-tracked Royal Mail service, then despatch a replacement same day. The bottom line is that the customer must not be inconvenienced more than is absolutely necessary – it's not their fault. They, quite rightly, see it as your responsibility to deliver the goods. You might end up losing money on that order (if you couldn't get compensation from the courier) but that is much better than having an angry customer.

3: If the customer has made a mistake

In our case, at least, this doesn't happen often. You can minimise the risk of this if you use a good quality ecommerce service with clear product information (including photos) an easily understood delivery policy, along with an order system that sends notifications when products are despatched.

Very occasionally we get customers who've confused themselves by looking at two sites at once, forgetting their address, not completing an order etc. Peta spends time interacting patiently with customers in these circumstances. Very rarely we have to conclude that we're not going to be able to help the customer for whatever reason – we have thousands of registered customers (people who created an account when they bought) and I think we've probably given up on perhaps 5. In some cases, the customer became rude[1] and in others it was clear, in the end, that we couldn't offer what they wanted.

Our default position, however, is that the fault lies with us unless it's obvious this isn't the case. Did the customer misunderstand something because we didn't make it clear enough? Could it have been a mistake by us or the courier?

For example, every now and again a customer will tell us their delivery hasn't arrived. Our policy is that, if it's now outside the delivery window, we immediately despatch a replacement by the quickest possible method. Just recently we did this and, after a few days, the customer complained that the replacement had also not arrived. So, we sent another – only to find that the customer had filled out their address wrongly (despite the fact that we'd asked her to confirm before sending the replacement).

So, we were two orders down, all due to the fact that a customer didn't know where she lived – we'd certainly lost money. However, in the vast majority of cases this approach of immediately despatching a replacement pays off and we end up with a happy customer and a refund from the courier. As it happened, in this case, we got one of the products back in the end.

In fact, how you deal with mistakes is at least as important as any other aspect of your business. By dealing honestly and fairly with the things that inevitably go wrong from time to time, you can transform an angry customer into one of your most avid and vocal supporters.

---

[1] There's a fine line between bending over backwards to help customers and allowing them to bully you. Never sacrifice your dignity or self esteem to abusive people – everyone deserves respect.

THE POWER OF REFERRAL

Treating customers fairly, over-delivering, dealing well with mistakes and focusing at least as much energy on pleasing existing customers as finding new ones – these things are critical to your marketing efforts.

What's all that got to do with marketing? Well, marketing is simply the process by which you connect your product with its target audience and encourage purchase. You'll use one set of techniques (including those listed above) to encourage existing customers to buy again and a different set to find new customers – the most familiar being advertising.

However, there is a form of marketing that is **much** more powerful than advertising – personal referral. After all, which would you give more weight to – a TV advert promoting a new product or the personal recommendation of a trusted friend?

As the owner of a craft business, you have another advantage – your products are advertising themselves in the homes of your customers! Whether you supply finished objects or kits, craft items are distinctive and attention grabbing and that includes everything from a gorgeous mantelpiece candle through a stunning piece of jewellery to the mouthwatering brownies that land on your customer's doormat.

HARNESSING RECOMMENDATIONS

Personal

The perfect recommendation is given by one friend to another. We often get emails from customers who tell us they were referred by someone they know but there's no easy method to measure how much of this is going on. The best you can do is to **ask** customers to recommend you to their friends and, if appropriate to your craft, give them something to hand on to them – perhaps a postcard with a voucher for a discount or free gift.

Reviews

Powerful though they are, personal recommendations are limited in their scope. Over time, as the number of customers you've served increases, so does your potential reach through this type of marketing. However, the vast majority of customers will find you by other means and will be looking for reassurance about the product they're considering buying.

By encouraging customers to give honest product reviews some time after purchasing, you're building up evidence visitors can use to validate their choice. Customers tend to buy non-essential products (and crafts do, just about, fall into that category) with their hearts. They buy it because they love it. However, they often need to keep the left-brain, analytical side of their nature satisfied also. If they see a dozen reviews of a product all giving a consistent verdict on its quality, the service they received and, in the case of kits, how easy they were to use, this helps to remove any doubt about the purchase.

It is easy to be cynical about reviews and there's no doubt that some companies and individuals write fakes, however I think most internet shoppers are beginning to develop a BS detector and a single dodgy review is probably enough to fatally undermine the company concerned in their mind. It is much better to have no reviews at all (after all, the customer may well think that the product is new to the market) than to have anything at all whiffy.

Most ecommerce systems have reviews built-into them and our system (based on BigCommerce) sends out an automatic reminder to all customers a couple of weeks after purchase asking them to review their product. We're notified of new reviews and we can then go into our back-office system and take a look. We have a policy of posting every review – whether good or bad – on the basis that this gives our reviews overall credibility. We do correct any horrendous spelling gaffes but otherwise reviews go up as posted. Very occasionally, a customer might have got entirely the wrong end of the stick, rendering their review more likely to confuse than help prospective customers. An example would be where a customer uses votive candle wax in a container candle and gives a negative review because the wax shrunk away from the edges (as it's designed to do so it can be released from the mould). If we get a review we can't publish for whatever reason, we contact the customer to see if we can resolve their issue. Overall, however, we publish and be damned!

Amazon relies heavily on reviews to publicise products and help with selection. When we sell a product through Amazon, these products can be reviewed in the usual way. But Amazon's main focus is on our performance as Marketplace sellers so they email customers after the product has arrived to ask how we did. This is used in all sorts of ways within the Amazon system but is also available to any potential buyer by simply clicking our name in the product listing.

My advice is to welcome reviews and feedback. You will get the occasional unreasonable or unfair review but, by and large, the crafting community and its customers are a pretty reasonable lot. As far as MakingYourOwnCandles is concerned, we attribute a large measure of our success to our open attitude to feedback and reviews, not just because we learn a lot about how customers see our products and service (which we can then use to improve both) but also because, whether or not a few cynical visitors suspect us of fiddling our reviews, we know we don't and I think, in the end, that comes across.

Social media
We're going to cover Facebook shortly – but one of its main purposes is to allow people to share their genuine thoughts on your services or products. It's great to receive photos of your products used in someone else's home, or the end results of a kit you've sent them. These sorts of posts are very valuable as they're not only clearly genuine but they

appear across the news feeds of many, many related people – lots of whom might never have heard of you before.

Rewards for referrals

We don't do this but, for some businesses, it'll make sense to offer existing customers a reward for recommending you. The reward should be proportionate and it should only be paid once the new customer has successfully placed an order. One option is to pick a small group of your very best customers and give them their own discount code. Most ecommerce systems allow you to specify that the code can only be used once per new customer so you can simply tot them up every month or so and pay the customer doing the referring based on how many new voucher claims there have been.

Now, I appreciate that if you give a 10% discount to the new customer and a 10% discount to the existing customer, this reduces your profit on that first order. But you've acquired a new customer without having to spend any other money on marketing – and that customer has been recommended, making them all the more likely to become multiple buyers.

Try to think of a customer in terms of their long term value to you. There are many businesses who plan to lose money on the first sale because they know they'll make a profit on later sales. Personally, I don't go in for that sort of business practice and there's no reason for any craft business to do it. However, please remember that, on average, the first purchase a customer makes is less profitable than later ones because these have a minimal marketing cost. You can use this saved money to offer discounts to existing customers so that they are treated well whilst you are still able to make a fair markup on your sales. Everyone's a winner.

The List

So, existing customers are valuable partly because they can "champion" you to their friends and family and also because it costs less to sell a second, third or fourth, product to them than it does to attract an entirely new customer.

By far the most powerful way to market to existing customers is via an email list. Other methods, including social media, have come along but nothing challenges a good email list for effectiveness.

Get Them on the List

More often than not, customers join your email list before they make their first process. Indeed, getting them on the list should be a key part of your marketing strategy.

The trick is to give potential customers a compelling reason to sign up. There was a time, a few years ago, when it was enough to promise some free information but that's unlikely to be the case now. You need a good inducement to buy the right to send occasional (and very profitable) emails and that will cost money but it's money well spent.

In our case, we offer 10% off a customer's first purchase and a free mini-kit. The cost to us is a small reduction in our profit margin on the first purchase and/or the small cost of the kit – a kit that has been specifically created to be low in cost to us and high in value to the customer. A series of emails is sent to the new potential customer introducing the craft of candle making – this also has the effect of reminding them about us over the next couple of weeks.

After that, they hear from us around once per month. They can unsubscribe at any time at all (your list should only include people who want to be on it) but, in our experience, very few do as long as you continue to provide interesting, useful emails and don't email too often.

We have thousands of people on our list at any one time – I actively manage the list by removing people if they've been on it for a couple of years without ever opening an email. The messages we send are only partly commercial, we also include hints, links to projects and news but their purpose is usually to encourage people to visit our Special Offer page. Think of the value of that list – thousands of customers and potential customers who've given us permission to email them. A well crafted email with interesting and relevant special offers will always result in a big bump in our sales on the day it's sent and for many days afterwards.

HOW TO DO IT

There are a number of email list services and I've used all the major ones (including aWeber and GetResponse) but I recommend MailChimp wholeheartedly (find a link at www.yourcraftbusiness.co.uk). Not least because it offers a very generous Free membership level which covers you for up to 2,000 subscribers.

Using MailChimp, you create a list and a signup form that you put in your online shop or website – it's very simple and quick to do. What happens is that when a visitor enters their email address (plus any other detail you've decided to capture – I recommend asking for their first name so you address emails personally) MailChimp sends them an email asking them to confirm their subscription (this is called "double opt-in" and is used to protect users from spam). If they click the link in that email, they'll be signed up and will receive your first email - usually containing information on how to claim their freebie or discount.

You can then use MailChimp to send a sequence of emails (an "autoresponder") to your new subscribers if you choose, and also to broadcast a message to your entire list.

When you come to broadcast a message to your list, make sure you create specific coupon codes for the special offers so you learn which sorts of deals your email customers respond best to.

A FEW "DON'TS"

Don't send people too many emails that are nothing more than sales letters. If enough recipients mark the email as "spam" your account will be suspended.

Don't be stingy with your sign-up offer. This is a common error – your offer must be attractive enough to get a good proportion of visitors signing up. I heard one marketer say that if the thought of giving so much away isn't hurting, you're not giving enough away. Perhaps that's a bit strong but you want them to instantly fill the form in (strike while the iron's hot) so the offer must be compelling

Don't, on the other hand, forget your list – email them at least monthly with something interesting, even if it's just your latest news. Even if all your email does is remind people that you exist, this, in itself, is useful marketing.

MARKETING TO NEW ONLINE CUSTOMERS

There are two common methods of finding new customers online: Pay Per Click advertising and Search Engine Optimisation.

PPC

Pay Per Click advertising does exactly what it says – you pay for each click on your ad. Google's AdWords programme is by far and away the most important platform and it's almost always the case that, if you want to use PPC, you'll start with them.

If you type "hand made soap" into Google.co.uk, you'll see ads along the top and down the side of the search results page. These have been created using AdWords. If you were to click on an ad, you'd be taken to the advertiser's page (usually an online shop) and they'd be charged for that click.

This is not a book about AdWords (there are plenty of those around) and PPC is one area where a little knowledge can be a dangerous thing. I strongly advise that you do not plunge head first into Google's tender embrace. It will do its best to convince you that if you just use its automatic settings and judgement to run your campaign, you'll do alright. This is very, very dangerous. If you decide to drive traffic to your site using PPC then you need to decide whether you want to learn enough to do it yourself or hire someone to do it.

A basic book on AdWords (such as Google AdWords for Dummies) will provide you with all the information you need to effectively manage your campaign. It's not that AdWords is hideously complicated at our level, it certainly isn't. It's just that it is completely unfamiliar so you need to go through some orientation before tackling it – or outsource it to someone else.

Why bother?

You might well be wondering what the point is – after all you went into business to create craft products, not become a pointy-headed marketing geek. The reason is simple – Google AdWords, used properly, is the single most potent way to bring buying customers into your store quickly.

PPC is like switching on a tap – right from the first hour after you start your campaign you can have targeted customers walking through your virtual front door. AdWords allows you to set up "conversion tracking" so that you can see which adverts are working best and how much they're costing you per transaction.

For example, let's say you sell rug making supplies. You create an ad that displays when the user types "latch hook rug making" into Google and 100 people click on it at a cost of 20p per click. Your total cost during that period was, therefore, £20 (100 x 20p). Of those 100 visitors to your site, four of them purchased kits (a 4% conversion rate) worth a total value of £200.

So, your cost per conversion was £5 (the £20 spend divided by 4 purchases) and the average purchase was £50 (the £200 total spend divided by 4 purchases) – in other words you spent around 10% of the value of the products in marketing them. The real issue is how much profit did you make? Well, it's pretty obvious that if you only spent £5 bringing in a sale of £50, your marketing is doing well if you use the True Cost + 75% model.

In fact, you can now adjust your pricing by including an accurate marketing percentage in your true cost calculation and, in that way, know that you will always be making a 75% margin as long as the 10% figure holds true.

Now, in that example, it's pretty obvious that PPC is paying its way. When you start a new campaign you always set a low daily budget (I stick to £5 per day) and work on it until it becomes profitable. The beauty of doing it this way is that you can now increase your budget and be pretty sure you'll continue to make the same margin on a much higher level of traffic (although you'd be well advised to keep a close watch on it!).

We've been running profitable PPC campaigns since we first started MakingYourOwnCandles.co.uk in 2009 and, to this day, it contributes the majority of our traffic. You can be sure that it more than pays its way and that I keep a very close eye on it. I suggest that most online shops will benefit from an effective AdWords campaign and, once you have a product range and online home that works well, it is usually worth at least giving it a try (on a low daily budget).

I recommend AdWords for Dummies as a starting point (link at
www.yourcraftbusiness.co.uk). You'll react in one of two ways. If you
get excited at the idea of creating a controllable stream of customers
for your virtual store then go ahead, learn how to do it and get stuck in.
If your eyes glaze over and the process of researching keywords,
writing ad copy and running experiments fills you with dread, then
think about getting someone in to help or, if you decide PPC isn't for
you, simply accept that your traffic levels will be lower, at least in the
short term. PPC almost always results in extra traffic – the issue is
whether the cost of that traffic is profitable to you.

SEARCH ENGINE OPTIMISATION
The good news is that there's another way to drive consistent traffic to
your online shop, and it's free (at least, it doesn't cost money – it
certainly takes time). You've probably had emails from SEO "experts"
promising you a front page position and my strong recommendation is
to ignore the lot of them. There are plenty of good SEO companies out
there and they don't spam potential customers – if you decide to use
one, go looking for them. After all, if you can't find them in Google, it
doesn't say much for their SEO skills does it?

But the big secret the SEO industry doesn't want you to know is that it's
actually very simple, at least in principle, to rank well in Google. As with
PPC, this isn't a book about SEO specifically, but I'll give you enough
information to decide how involved in it you want to be.

Let's go back to our rug kit maker – Reggie's Rugs. Naturally, Reggie
wants to appear on page 1 of the search results. Hold on, though, what
does that actually mean? It's only worthwhile being on the first page if
people searching for rugs see it. So, the first thing to do is work out
which search phrases you want to rank well for.

In Reggie's case, he wants to appear on page 1 for "latch hook kits" and
a selection of other related search phrases. Here's the important point:
the more specific and "long tail" the search phrase, the easier it is to get
on page 1, the better the quality of the traffic arriving at your site but
that traffic will be lower in volume. You need to decide which search
phrase you want to rank well for, before you start your SEO work.

There are, broadly speaking, two main factors Google uses when it ranks your site: the site content and the quality/quantity of sites linking to it. The first of these you can handle yourself very easily. If you're using any of the recommended approaches to getting your website up and running, Google will have no technological problem adding your site to its index. You can use these tools to edit the pages of your site to make sure they include your search terms. There was a time, years ago, when you would stuff the page full of them and you'd be rewarded with a good position but this is no longer the case – indeed if you do this you're more likely to be punished or even removed entirely from the index of sites.

The sorts of changes I mean are:

- use your search phrase in your page title. For example "Reggie's Rugs – Latch Hook Rug Kits"

- use your search phrase in your headings and body text

- when you add photos of the kits, make sure their description includes the search phrase.

You get the picture- the idea is that Google is in no doubt what the page is about. Reggie should organise his site so that all his Latch Hook kits are on one category page, and similarly with the other key phrases.

It's all about links

When it comes to a high ranking, however, links are the most important aspect. So, it's essential to get other relevant sites to link to you – Google will only reward you if it thinks the link comes from a site that's related. The theory is that if a lot of relevant sites link to your website, this gives it more weight ("authority" in SEO speak) and pushes it up the rankings.

The good news is that in low competition markets, you don't need many links at all to appear high up the rankings. You can get these links by joining a craft organisation or having your site listed in a craft directory. You can also do this by starting and running your own blog as I described in the last chapter.

ONE MORE THING

I talked, right at the beginning, about the importance of getting your business name right. This needs to be reflected in the domain address. As I explained, MakingYourOwnCandles.co.uk was chosen for very good SEO reasons. All other things being equal, www.reggieslatchhookrugkits.co.uk will outrank www.reggiesrugs.co.uk for a user searching on "latch hook rug kits".

PATIENCE

The reason many people start with PPC is that it generates instant results. SEO, on the other hand, can take weeks or months to have an effect. This is not least because Google penalises new sites – a year-old site will always outrank an identical week-old site. It also takes time to get the links in place and for these changes to filter through. Once done, however, your Google search ranking is capable of delivering a regular stream of traffic to your site for free. Ignore it at your peril.

FACEBOOK

For most craft businesses, whether they sell online or exclusively at craft fairs, Facebook is likely to be the best social media choice. Twitter is widening its appeal amongst craft customers but doesn't allow you to create the sense of community that lies at the heart of your social marketing. It may well be that Google+ becomes a credible alternative in the coming months and years (I love it personally) but, for now, it tends to be largely inhabited by bearded pointy-heads (like me).

COMMUNITY

Earlier in this chapter I talked about referrals and recommendations – Facebook comments and status updates are an example of this. Ideally, you want to foster a community where fans of the page add their own updates and photos and interact with each other. By doing this, you become synonymous with your chosen craft as far as that group of people is concerned.

First and foremost, make sure you start a Facebook Page – not a Group and you certainly shouldn't use a personal account. Once you've got it set up and populated with a few stories and photos, encourage your Facebook friends to "like" it. This will then show up on the news feeds of all *their friends,* giving you instant exposure.

WHAT TO POST

Facebook likes photos – the Timeline view introduced in 2011 is built around photography. So, where at all possible, post photos rather than just text updates.

Your fans want to hear what you're up to on a day to day basis, so updates about what new products you're working on, or the challenges of running your own craft business are usually very welcome. They won't want to be deluged with sales pitches – this is the quickest way to being "unliked".

You can add quick polls/quizzes and videos, as well as bringing the attention of your fans to other happenings in the crafting world. You should also promote any craft fairs by setting them up as Events on your page and offering an incentive for your Facebook friends to attend.

The purpose is to give the page and community a life of its own – to be somewhere people want to spend time and interact with others who share the same interest. Crafters are passionate people, but (especially those interested in more obscure crafts) they might well struggle to find others locally to share their passion – that's what Facebook is for.

THE BOTTOMLESS PIT

You probably know that Facebook floated on the US stock exchange recently. The problem they now have is that shareholders will expect to see a return on their investment and, just like Google (and Twitter and LinkedIn), they see advertising as the way to achieve this. On the positive side, this means they're coming up with ever more innovative ways you can use to promote yourself to your audience. However, the flip side of this is that many of these methods have yet to prove themselves effective for small businesses so you need to tread very carefully indeed.

Many of the best promotional features are reserved for pages with 400 fans or more. This is Facebook's attempt to prevent spammers and other chancers from polluting the social network. So your initial target should be to get up to 400 fans and the quickest way to do this is likely to be via advertising. A "page like" ad, pops up in the right hand column of Facebook whenever someone likes your page – their friends see something like "Kevin Liked MakingYourOwnCandles" which encourages them to take a look. This works quite well for growing an audience and you should expect to spend 20p-40p per new like. This can mount up pretty quickly but bear in mind that each of those new fans has friends of their own so you might find that it's just necessary to give the page a boost (adding, say, 100 fans at a cost of £30) and then writing lots of good content that encourage their friends to like the page too.

Once you get up to 400 fans you can then use "promoted posts" to get a prominent position on the news feeds of all your fans.

My general advice is that PPC advertising is more likely to bring buying customers to your shop (Facebook advertising, after all, generally advertises Facebook pages) and that is where your initial efforts should lie. However if, for whatever reason, you decide not to go down that route, it's worth working out whether you can base your marketing around Facebook.

How will you know if it's worth it? Simply by creating discount coupons that you only publicise on Facebook – use either a simple status update or one of the many forms of Facebook advertising to promote the coupons and see how many people bite -and at what cost (if any).

In our case, we love our Facebook community but its commercial value is relatively low – AdWords remains our primary traffic source.

OLD FASHIONED PAPER PROMOTION

There's a good reason I'm dealing with these methods last – it's because they are often entirely ineffective. The first thing a lot of new businesspeople consider when they think about advertising their business is Yellow Pages, classified ads, business cards and flyers.

YELLOW PAGES/YELL.COM AND SIMILAR DIRECTORIES

You're not a plumber, and my advice is to steer clear of any and all paper-based advertising like this and their associated online directories. At some point, you're likely to get a phone call, email or letter from one or more of them. They'll tell you that they represent a great way of advertising and, after all, your competitors will be on there, shouldn't you be?

Think about this – when was the last time you search on yell.com for anything, let alone a craft business? Where do you go? Google, in all likelihood. And this is why I recommend most craft businesses concentrate their efforts on Google and Facebook.

The "local" argument no longer holds any water either – if you serve a local community, you can register your business via Google+ Local and there's a good chance it'll appear when a potential customer who lives nearby searches for you. And this is all free of charge. My advice is to save your marketing money for a more genuinely worthwhile use.

CLASSIFIED ADS/MAGAZINE ADVERTISING

This form of advertising is also going the way of the dinosaurs, at least for businesses like ours. Whether local or via craft magazines, I see no evidence that they're effective. The problem with advertising of this sort is that you need to shell out the money upfront without knowing if the campaign will be effective. Sure, that magazine may have 50,000 readers per month, but how many will even **see** your ad as they flick through, let alone read it, much less **act on it**.

If they're reading a craft magazine and get a hankering to give that craft a go they're likely to either plump straight for the craft company that featured in the article (or sponsored it- beware this too) or they'll pop over to Google on their iPad and search. Again, this is where you need to be – in the electronic world, not on paper. Having said that, if you have a physical location you sell from, then advertising in the local parish magazine is cheap and at least you're doing your bit for the community.

Business Cards

These **are** worth having – whether you operate in the "real world" of craft fairs or the virtual world. One way or another, you are going to meet people and the business card is the traditional way to swap details. If you're relying mainly on real world events then you'll need a much bigger supply of cards, however!

VistaPrint seems to be the default choice of many for business cards but I recommend Moo (uk.moo.com). You can upload your own design (especially if you've followed "Design for Non-Designers") or choose and adapt one of the large range of good quality designs. You can then order in quantities are low as 50 cards – although the more you order at any one time, the less it costs per card.

It's worth taking time to get the design right – you should make the effort to upload your logo to properly personalise the cards. Outside the digital world, business cards are often the first impression a potential customer has of you – particularly if they've been handed it by a third party.

Flyers

Again, lots of people immediately think of paper flyers when they think of business advertising. Now, as long as you have a definite and worthwhile purpose in mind, they can be powerful – especially if you can hand them out at craft-fairs or other events your audience might attend.

As with other aspects of design, please get them done nicely. By all means, if you have graphical talent (or have read the aforementioned book) give it a go – and don't be ashamed to do a Google image search for "craft flyer" to see what other people are doing. Remember, though, this isn't about ripping other designs off, it's about understanding current trends and triggering your imagination.

Printed.com is a good place to have them printed once done – my view is that if you're going to have flyers made, you should print them in colour, even if that means you can afford fewer. As with so many other marketing issues, it's about quality – getting your gorgeous leaflets in front of the right people, rather than having a black and white version shoved into the local newspaper.

Case Study: Littlecote Soap Co (www.littlecotesoap.co.uk)

How do you promote your business?

"We now attend trade shows and have optimised our website very well for our keywords, which brings in the business that we require. We also advertise in our local parish newsletter, and still attend a few local events to promote our business. We found that the best way to advertise our business was to get out there and show people our products. We found that paying for advertising was costly, and not particularly effective, unless you spend a huge amount, although local Parish Magazines are good value and are often worth doing. We also issue press releases to the local newspaper about new products, or you could just contact the Editor of your local paper to let them know about yourself, they are always looking for interesting stories, you could offer a giveaway of your product in return for a free editorial."

The key with marketing is to remember its purpose – to bring your product and its customers together. Effective marketing does this at a price that means you make a profit on the sales it generates. Never, never lose sight of the importance of being able to measure whether the marketing you pay for works. There are plenty of providers of promotional materials and advertising media who would like you to forget that but you're not a big corporation, content to chuck money at advertising in the hope that some of the mud sticks. You're a lean, mean, microbusinessperson and every penny has to earn its keep.

MILESTONE 6: YOUR MARKETING PLAN

Marketing needs proper planning: which of the many forms of marketing are you going to concentrate on? In almost every case, you will want to spend at least a little time on SEO – it's very easy and it takes time to have an effect so you need to get started early.

Do you want a fast start to your online business? Then consider Pay Per Click advertising via AdWords.

However you intend to promote your business, write down a clear marketing plan that involves doing a little every day, or every few days. Don't try to do it all in one go. And remember, marketing comes *after* you've created your product line, not before. Sausage before sizzle every time.

Chapter 12: The Secrets of Running A Successful Business

Well, you've reached the end of the book – congratulations. Although there's certainly a lot to learn and do if you want to set up your own craft business, I hope that by now you've been convinced of three things:

1. It isn't rocket science – it's a process

2. It isn't about luck – it's about carefully finding the right combination of products, marketplace and marketing and then running an efficient business.

3. You can do it – if you've got this far you clearly have the stamina, I am confident you have the talent. So if you can do it, you really should do it. You owe it to yourself.

Here are the most important lessons Elaine from The Littlecote Soap Co has learned since starting her business 9 years ago:

> *"You will never be able to make a product that absolutely everyone likes. Don't be offended or rude to customers if they give you constructive criticism even if you think it is not appropriate. Say that you will take it on board and think about it later to see if they have any valid points. However, do not be too quick to make changes just on the back of one comment, don't forget the hundreds of other customers that are perfectly satisfied with your product. If your products are not selling well in the location that you are selling them, then perhaps it is the location, or the target market, that is not suited to your products, so try a different tack."*

And here's what Anita from SayItWithBrownies.co.uk had to say:

> *"The single thing I underestimated was the difficulty in attracting customers. I had the impression that people would just find my site on google, but with so many websites out there this was very naïve of me. I had a couple of breaks early on, a chocolate reviewer wrote a lovely review about my Cookies & Cream Brownies and a local newspaper wrote and article about me. Twitter has been amazing and I quickly got into the swing of using it. The other key lesson is the importance of gaining local support. Initially I played down the*

fact that I am based on the Isle of Wight as I thought it might put potential customers off with concerns about the post taking longer. But I soon changed my mind as islanders were incredibly supportive. I now shout loudly about being based here and do anything I can to support other island businesses in the same way."

As a reward for making it this far, I'm going to rattle off 7 lessons Peta, myself and other successful craft business-owners have learned.

1: Organise for Success

Peta is the most organised person I know. Which is fortunate because I'm the least organised person I know. She has set up her workshop to suit her – both in terms of assembling orders and so that she can keep an eye on stock levels and order in plenty of time.

Organisation is absolutely critical to keeping the number of mistakes you make to a bare minimum. No-one is perfect but having a (neatly labelled) place for everything and everything in its (neatly labelled) place makes this much easier. This isn't easy for everyone - I suspect that if I were in charge it'd be chaotic within days, despite the fact that I know how important it is. We each have our strengths but, in a business that depends on the efficient managing of orders, organisations is an under-rated but critical skill.

2: Love your Customers

I am not exaggerating when I say that we adore our customers. The vast majority are simply lovely. Despite fulfilling thousands and thousands of orders since 2009 we can still hardly believe that people not only buy our products but also react so positively to them. This spurs us on to continue to do even better.

We've come across very, very few nasty customers. We've had problems caused by confusion and the occasional daftness (on both sides) but we could count the number of customers we've been forced to sack because they weren't prepared to treat Peta respect on the fingers of one hand. Which is pretty good going.

We therefore treat all customer complaints as if they were genuine (they usually are) and do our absolute utmost to make them happy.

Frankly, if we saw customers as our enemies we wouldn't enjoy our work and we probably wouldn't be very good at it. Makingyourowncandles is a nice place to work.

Your customers, far more than your products, are your true resource. Look after them.

3: Keep Your Eyes On The Money

Cashflow kills more businesses than anything else once they're up and running. If you're used to balancing the family books you have a head start but the main temptation to avoid is taking money out of the business too early. In the early days it makes sense to leave it there either as a buffer against unexpected bills or an unusually quiet period, or use it to build up a bigger stock of products.

This is critical – make sure that every single thing you spend money on pays its way. Be tough with yourself. This is why we don't have a white van with our logo on – we use our family car to lump mailsacks (sometimes a dozen at a time) to the sorting office. Emotionally, we love the idea of having our own van but it cannot possibly pay its own way so we haven't got one, even though we could afford it. Every penny must pay.

Even expenses such as your monthly FreeAgent subscription pays its way because it usually removes the need to employ a book-keeper (or, at least, reduces the time your book-keeping takes someone else to do). Your job is to sniff out any expenses that are unnecessary – this means looking for value for money in everything you do (which isn't necessarily the cheapest).

As your business expands, there's a natural temptation to ease off on this. But you mustn't – the bigger you get, the more will be wasted by making poor choices and the bigger the problems if you have a cashflow squeeze.

Ask yourself, with every decision you make "where's the money?"

4: MULTIPLE SOURCES OF INCOME

I think it's a mistake to rely on one income source – it's just too risky. Whilst our web shop generates most of our income, the fact that we also sell through Amazon and, sometimes, through eBay means that if any one of these is threatened (by, for example, a technical failure) we can still make some money.

This also applies to your product range. Once you have a core range in place, you can expand it outwards so that it reaches a wider audience. Adding kits to your range is one example of this – sometimes these additional products take off and you find yourself running a much more profitable business!

If you intend to sell largely at craft fairs, add an Amazon shop or a shopping cart to your website. This way, you can take advantage of the busy period up to Christmas so that you're earning even when you're not at a show.

Nail down your primary outlet first, then look to grow outwards.

5: BUILD A SUPPORT NETWORK

Running a business can be lonely. Some people appreciate the support of other, more experienced, business owners but the main help you'll need is from your family and friends. Whether that's in the form of being understanding about the hours you're working or through actually helping in the business, you're likely to need support from time to time.

In our case, Peta and I are lucky because we both work in the business. We're even more lucky because we have complementary skills so there's little overlap or cause for conflict. We also "hire in" family when we need help meeting demand – our components are outsourced to family members and, when things get really busy before Christmas, we have a house full of aunties, grandparents and children.

If there isn't anyone you can talk to about business, reach out to other crafters at your next fair or by email – the chances are they feel the same way.

6: BELIEF IS EVERYTHING

Starting up your own business puts you in a pretty exclusive club. Plenty of people have the idea of running their own business but only a small minority actually go through with it. This very fact means you are capable of running a successful business. There are no guarantees, least of all in business, but I can tell you that if you give it your best shot and if you're sensible with the amount of money you invest in the business, then, even if you decide in the end to stop trading, you can at least say that you did it. And that's a whole lot better than never giving it a try.

Your belief in yourself shines through in every aspect of your business – from the design of your products to the brilliance of your website and the confident handling of customers. The process outlined in this book is designed to give you ever more confidence that your product and business model is a winner. Sure, lots of businesses fail (although fewer than you might imagine) but many of those failures are by people who didn't go through the process in this book, they just winged it. By taking care to get your products right in the first place, you've overtaken most of your competitors. And remember, you haven't got to be perfect – you've just got to be better than them.

Never let anyone who hasn't started a business put you down. In fact, don't let anyone put you down full-stop. You've taken action, you've done something brave and admirable and you certainly shouldn't take any nonsense from armchair cynics!

7: NEVER GIVE UP, NEVER SURRENDER

What characteristic separates the success story from the also-ran? A bloody-minded refusal to let any obstacle get in their way. I'm not suggesting for one moment that you should continue flogging a dead horse if your business is never going to succeed but, on the other hand, it's rarely the case that a business is unsalvageable. If you've been through a well-thought out process of setting up your craft enterprise, it's more likely that you will find success with a change in direction (perhaps very minor) or a more effective marketing campaign.

Watch out for the direction of travel – are things getting better or not? It may be very slow and it may well be masked by seasonal variations (you can only really tell if a business is succeeding if a month's sales in year 2 are higher than the equivalent month in year 1) but is revenue increasing? Are you finding more customers? Is your website ranking higher this month than last? Direction is everything – spot a slowdown early enough and there's time to make a course correction.

When all's said and done, however, there's no great mystery to creating a great craft business. Make a great product and sell it – that's it. There's a lot behind that simple statement (and much of it is covered in this book) but that's the essence of it. You now know more than the vast majority of new business owners. I don't pretend that this book covers absolutely everything but, if you've followed along, you'll now have a quality product at a decent markup ready for sale. There's much still to be done but I hope this book has given you the important jumping-off points so that you can go ahead and get yourself set up with an online shop, for example.

You end this book ahead of the game – it's time to push on now and bring your business to life. I'm looking forward to seeing what you can do – surprise me.

ACKNOWLEDGMENTS

This book is dedicated to my wonderful wife Peta, without whom MakingYourOwnCandles wouldn't exist. This book was made possible by her loving support and encouragement.

I also want to thank my parents, Doug and Margaret, from the bottom of my heart. They supported my writing at its beginning, not least by paying for a correspondence course in the 1980s. They are at the heart of our wider family, providing a framework of unconditional love within which their children and grandchildren can flourish.

Finally, I'd like to thank the whole of my family for being the wonderful, loving bunch of nutters they are. And especially, my three children – Kirsty, Lucy and George for being the best things I ever had a role in creating.

3305583R00100

Printed in Great Britain
by Amazon.co.uk, Ltd.,
Marston Gate.